Life Force Energy

7 Ultimate Steps To Create Your Ideal Lifestyle

**By
Puneet Dixit**

First edition published by Puneet Dixit
www.LifeForceEnergyBook.com

Copyright © 2015 Puneet Dixit
ISBN: 978-1508952121

All rights reserved including the right of reproduction in whole or part in part in any form.

Preface

We are so much focused on our physical existence and the surrounding material reality, that we devote no time to self-introspection. We rather choose to ignore the valid questions that daunt our minds from time to time in our lives. Who we really are? Where did we come from? Is there some profound truth that lies behind the illusion of our physical existence? What is the ultimate purpose of our lives? Science explains to many things but only at the physical level.

Effort in seeking answers to these questions led me to explore and practice yogic philosophy for past decade and I came to realize that the fundamental block responsible for the existence and holding of the entire universe together is not matter but energy.

The foundation of life rests upon fundamental creative power or energy that is the source as well as the substance behind all existence. Experiencing this creative power within our physical being and consciously making efforts to unite with this infinite power takes us closer to our true self. The connection with the true self not only gratifies our curious minds but also helps us realize our true purpose and potential in life. Good health, longevity, success, healthy relationships, happiness and bliss are some of the by-products of realizing one's inner energy.

In this book I share with you some of the secrets, practices and knowledge that have helped me awaken and tap into this infinite life force energy that is available to us for free all the time. Universe doesn't charge us anything for using this energy that is available in abundance all the time. We only need to look within, learn a few practices to awaken the inner forces and make life pleasant and worth living. Awakening this energy will ultimately make you realize that miracles are plentiful as well as possible.

I have tried to precisely explain how the strengthening of our energy body can help us meet the daily challenges and achieve success in all spheres of life, ranging from career and finance to relationships and health.

This is a humble attempt to introduce you to a whole new experience of looking at life and enjoying it inside out!!

With lots of love,
Puneet Dixit

About the Author

Puneet Dixit is a yoga and meditation teacher and a life force energy coach. He comes from a holistic spiritual background in India born in the lineage of one of the Seven Vedic Sages Rishi Bhardwaj. He studied Yoga and Vedanta since early childhood from her Grandmother who was a Vedic and Sanskrit scholar. He is the founder of Higher Self Yoga which teaches people how to connect to their higher self and live in line with their higher purpose.

Puneet understands the principles with which life force energy operates and is on a mission to spread unconditional love and happiness in the lives of people. With a background in spirituality and a degree in Engineering and MBA he understands the challenges that the common man faces in day to day life and is always ready to help people with his gifts of healing with the energy of unconditional divine love.

He specializes in removing the energetic blockages that prevent people from achieving their goals in life. He has created a special program called *Awaken Your Inner Energy*. This course combines the best of ancient yogic teachings with the modern scientific and psychological techniques to achieve best of health happiness and harmony in life.

Life Force Energy

Dedicated to

The Cosmic intelligence that appears in the form of a Guru guiding us in our journey of life.

The Universal Energy which gives life to every form and matter that exists.

The all-pervading Cosmic Consciousness that makes the universe operational.

Life Force Energy

Acknowledgement

I like to thank Dr Jitendra Bhargava for his valuable support in reviewing and editing the book. I would also like to thank my wife Gunjan for her patience and support throughout the journey of bringing this book to life. I feel grateful to my entire family and loving friends for acting as a mirror so I can see my evolution and growth through them. Finally I would like to thank my Guru and the Divine Energy whom I worship as Mother as that is what has brought everything to life.

|| Om Shree Durgarpanamastu ||

Foreword

Dear Being of Energy,

You have the key to achieve all your dreams, all your goals and create a lifestyle that supports your ideal health, ideal wealth and ideal relationships. The KEY is in your energy or rather the LIFE FORCE ENERGY that is flowing through you. This book teaches you precisely how to work with your energy at each level of its manifestation, in the form of food, air, sound, money, emotions and thoughts.

When you surround your self with great positive energy, great things happen and the same is true for this book. As Puneet says in this book that everything is energy, so is this book. I am sure that the life force energy of this book will be of great help to you to turn around your life and create your ideal life style that is full of energy, love and enthusiasm. By reading each chapter and doing the suggested exercises you can transform your energy which will transform your life.

This book will be of great help to everyone and will inspire many to explore and develop understanding of their very own life force energy that is with them always, all the time.

Pay careful attention to what Puneet presents in this important book. Your ideal lifestyle depends on it.

Raymond Aaron
New York Times Best-Selling Author
Raymond is the author of Double Your Income Doing What You Love, Chicken Soup for the Canadian Soul and many other

bestselling books. He is known as the #1 success and investment coach, teaching people just like you how to use his goal setting strategies to change your life.

Contents

INTRODUCTION: WHAT IS LIFE FORCE ENERGY? **17**
    LIFE FORCE ENERGY EQUATION 20

CHAPTER 1: ENERGY FROM FOOD **23**
    CALORIE VS LIFE FORCE ENERGY OF FOOD 25
    SUN AS THE ULTIMATE SOURCE OF ENERGY 30
    HOW DID YOU COOK YOUR FOOD? 31
    EAT INTUITIVELY 32
    MINDFUL EATING VS MOUTHFUL EATING 33
    HOW MUCH TO EAT 35
    BLESSING THE FOOD INCREASES ITS LIFE FORCE ENERGY 36

CHAPTER 2: ENERGY FROM BREATH **37**
    SCIENCE OF BREATHING 38
    LIFE FORCE ENERGY OF BREATH 39
    BREATH AND MIND 40
    YOGIC BREATHING 42
    BENEFITS OF YOGIC BREATHING 46
    THE TWO NOSTRILS, YIN AND YANG AND THE TWO HEMISPHERES OF BRAIN 47

CHAPTER 3: ENERGY FROM CHAKRAS **51**
    THE 7 CHAKRAS AND THEIR LOCATION 54
    ANATOMY OF CHAKRAS 55
    MOOLADHAR CHAKRA 58
    SWADHISTHAN CHAKRA 59
    MANIPURA CHAKRA 60
    ANAHAT CHAKRA 61
    VISHUDDHI CHAKRA 62
    AJNA CHAKRA 63
    SAHASRAR CHAKRA 64

CHAPTER 4: THOUGHTS AS ENERGY 65

HAPHAZARD THINKING = LOSS OF ENERGY 67
HOW I CREATED THOUGHT CONTROL 67
CREATING REALITY WITH THOUGHTS 69
YOU ARE NOT YOUR THOUGHTS 71
POWER OF COMPANY 74
HOW TO CONTROL YOUR THOUGHTS 75
EXERCISE: TRATAKA 77

CHAPTER 5: EMOTIONS AS ENERGY 79

THE RIGHT WAY TO DEAL WITH THE ENERGY OF EMOTIONS 80
ENERGY OF LOVE 81
STORY OF NACHIKETA 82
EMOTIONAL BLOCKAGES 83
HOW TO CONNECT TO YOUR FEELINGS 83
EMOTIONS AND CHAKRAS 84
MOOLADHAR OR SURVIVAL CENTRE 85
SWADHISTHAN THE PASSION CENTRE 85
MANIPURA THE POWER CENTRE 85
ANAHAT THE HEART CENTRE 86
VISHUDDHI THE SELF EXPRESSION CENTRE 86
AJNA THE DECISION CENTRE 86
SAHASRAR THE SPIRITUAL CENTRE 87
MEDITATION TO RELEASE BLOCKED EMOTIONS 87

CHAPTER 6: WORDS AS ENERGY 91

DR EMOTO'S WORDS ARE ALIVE WATER EXPERIMENT 94
AFFIRMATIONS 94
LOSS OF ENERGY 96
ENERGY OF VISHUDDHI (THROAT) CHAKRA: UNINHIBITED SELF
EXPRESSION 97
NEVER COMPLETE A NEGATIVE SENTENCE ABOUT YOURSELF OR OTHERS
.... 98

CULTIVATING AWARENESS OF SPEECH 99
ENERGY OF SOUND – MANTRAS 101
EXERCISE: MAUNA 102

CHAPTER 7: MONEY AS ENERGY 103

MYTHS ABOUT MONEY 104
MONEY IS THE ENERGETIC MEANS AND NOT THE END 105
ALIGN MONEY WITH LOVE 106
YOUR CHAKRAS ARE BLOCKING YOUR MONEY ENERGY 107
YOUR KARMIC PATTERNS ARE BLOCKING YOUR MONEY ENERGY ... 108
ALLOW THE ENERGY TO FLOW 109
EXERCISE: BLESS YOUR MONEY 110

CONCLUSION: TRANSFORMING YOUR ENERGY 113

TIPS ON MEDITATION 116

I CAN HELP YOU!! 119

TESTIMONIALS 121

AWAKEN YOUR INNER ENERGY 125

FROM CHAOS TO PEACE 127

CHAKRA HEALING 129

CHAKRA HEALING SESSION 129

AURIC CLEARING 131

AURIC CLEARING SESSION 131

RAISE YOUR MONEY ENERGY 133

KARMIC PATTERNS HEALING 135

KARMIC HEALING SESSION 135

FREE BONUSES 137

Life Force Energy

Introduction:
What is Life Force Energy?

Everything Is Energy

Albert Einstein shocked the world when he gave the famous equation

$$E=MC^2$$

Life Force Energy

Prior to Einstein, the world saw matter and energy as two separate things. Einstein showed that the matter and energy are inseparable and interchangeable. When this energy is vibrating at a very slow rate then we perceive it as matter. This means that everything is in essence energy and that the entire world is a manifestation of energy only. The yogis have been saying the same thing since aeons in the form of poetic verses mentioned in the yoga sutras, the Vedas and the Upanishads. In fact according to ancient yogic texts our psychophysical existence is due to this very energy in various forms. Our physical body is made of energy. However, what we experience through this physical body in the form of thoughts, feelings and emotions is also energy. They give this energy the name of Prana or Life Force Energy. It is this energy that is the force of our life. As a result of this energy we are alive and experience the beautiful gift Life day in and day out. Every moment we are floating in this soup of energy and trying to attract, create and add more energy that we can call our own in the form of money, house, car and other physical possessions or in the form of happy relationships that give meaning to life.

Prana form of life force energy is what creates and constitutes the entire universe. It is present in everything that moves and even things that do not move. We extract and exchange this life force energy from our environment. Chinese call this energy as Chi and in the Japanese culture it is referred to as Ki. If we don't get enough Prana or life force energy, we start degenerating in our physical as well as mental and emotional dimensions. So it is very important that we ingest only the purest of elements that supply us this energy such as pure food, pure water, and pure air. This life force energy exists in all living elements. However, due to social conditioning, most people know very little about it and how the same can be extracted from the environment to lead an energetic life. You might ask, "Does this Life Force Energy called Prana really exist?" Here is an interesting and scientific observation. People were weighed just before death and when weighed again a moment after they had died, it was found that they had lost about six ounces. What accounts for this weight loss? The researchers believe that it is the loss of our vital Life Force Energy at the instant of death that accounts for this weight loss. The human body emanates this energy and a bioelectric force field exists referred as Aura.

Scientists describe this as bio plasma and measure its sphere of influence just as they would do for any other force field. In USA, Dr. Burr and Northrop of Yale have mapped and measured the emanation of this energy body using sensitive voltmeters. In one of their experiment they connected the voltmeters to two trees and recorded the fluctuations in their life-fields over a period of many years. Kirilian photography is another famous way of scientifically seeing the aura or bio energy of objects and humans. Dr. Thelma Moss reported that Kirilian photographs of fresh, healthy leaves show a pattern of bubbles and veins in the interior and a radiation flaring beyond the leaf itself. In another famous experiment what investigators did was that they cut away one third of a leaf, yet the Kirilian photo showed the whole leaf intact. The energy pattern of the whole leaf persisted in spite of being cut into two. This is called the phantom leaf effect and is also reported by amputees feeling and sensing a phantom limb. In fact Kirilian photographs of the full healthy leaf and when the leaf was cut also show remarked difference in the colour of the auric field around the leaf. The aura of healthy leaf was aqua blue in colour. When the leaf was cut the aura of the entire leaf turned bloody maroon red. Thus we see the bioplasmic body of the leaf, like Burr's L-field is exactly what the yogis claim to be life force energy or Prana.

In effect we human beings are energy intensive organisms; we extract energy, we store it, and we use it up. The life force energy enters our body in the form of food and water that we consume, it enters and leaves our body through the air we breathe and interestingly what most people don't know it also enters our body through seven main energy centres called Chakras that are present in our life force energy body. We will discuss more about these chakras in the coming chapters but for the moment you can visualise that a huge amount of life force energy that sustains you comes into your body through these energy centres called Chakras. In fact you will be amazed to know as to how much energy we receive from these Chakras.

Do you want to know? Ok let me tell you. According to Siddha-Yogis we receive only 10% of the life force energy through the food we eat, Shocked !! We receive only 20% of the life force energy from the air we breathe Another Shock !! And finally the Chakras of which most people have no clue are responsible for 70% of the life force energy... BLOWN AWAY !! And yet most of the humanity is fighting over the 10% component of the life sustaining life force energy. May be that is why the yogis can live without food or air for long periods of time, because they know how to tap the 70% component through Chakras that keeps you alive.

Based on the above The Einstein's famous energy equation can be extended to cover the psycho-physical realities that we experience as humans.

Life Force Energy Equation

The Psychophysical Equation of Life Force Energy: -

Energy Intake   Energy Usage
$10F + 20B + 70C$ = Emotions + Thoughts + Words + Actions

Your RESULTS are based on your *Intake* and *Usage* of this Life Force Energy equation.

So, we intake life force energy through our food, our breath and our chakras. We spend this energy through the emotions we feel, the thoughts we think, the words we speak, and, the actions we perform. For most people, the two sides are unequal and highly imbalanced. What I mean by this is that most people firstly do not know how to effectively intake the life force energy with the result that they constantly survive in an energy depleted state. Or even if they are aware, their focus is only on the 10% component of energy in the form of food. I mean how many of you have practiced special exercises to improve your breathing?

Some of you might have heard about Chakras but how many of you have really done something to make sure that they stay healthy and open to supply sources of life force energy available to us?

Now coming to the other side of the equation let us see how most of us are spending this energy. With every thought you think and every emotion you experience you are spending the valuable life force energy. It is not just when you are speaking or doing something with your physical body that you spend energy. Life force energy is what is what fuels your mind and emotions. It affects your physical, mental and emotional states. The mental and emotional bodies are subtler than the physical body but all the more are more powerful. For example, physical reactions of emotions such as anger or fear are instances of the emotional body taking over the physical body. And of course, all of you must have experienced how positive thoughts uplift our actions and negative thoughts cause adverse physical reactions, gestures, speech and productivity.

And then there is another problem. For most people the other side of equation is also haphazardly organized. What I mean by this is that they are feeling one thing, thinking about something else, speaking yet another thing and doing something totally different. Isn't that true? How many times have you spent your life force energy or rather wasted it by misaligning these four components. And that is what manifests in the form of results that you get in your life like how much money you are making, or how good health you are enjoying or how beautiful and amazing relationships you have.

It is all manifestation of the life force energy, how much of it you are in-taking and how you are spending it. Now imagine how much powerful you can become if you align the components involved in the spending of this energy. If your thoughts, emotions, words and actions are properly aligned you can achieve a major positive shift in your results. Wouldn't you?

Lets explore this equation in the coming chapters and learn how to optimise results with life force energy. Lets take a deep dive into each of these components in the coming chapters and see how to create an ideal lifestyle by utilising life force energy in an optimum manner.

So Let's Begin!

Chapter 1:
Energy from Food

Do you want to achieve optimum health not just physically but mentally and emotionally as well by optimizing the life force energy of the food?

Do you know there is more to the energy of the food you eat than just its nutritional value?

In this age of super fast cars, super fuels and smart phones, people are suffering from acute personal energy crisis. They are constantly fatigued, full of tension, anxiety, stress and depression. Despite the fascination with diet programs and 'super energy foods', we have lost the formula for fundamental physical vitality. People switch between either a complete disregard for what they eat or a fanatical obsession with nutrients such as proteins, vitamins, minerals and calories. Popular culture is to eat more and more of food that makes us addictive to taste, unhealthy and energy draining food rather than the one for enriching and uplifting. And even the food that you might label as conventionally healthy due to the nature of how it is being processed it loses its energetic value although its calorific value might be preserved. It doesn't add to the energetic value that you would expect it to add in terms of you feeling rejuvenated, lighter in your mind, and, freer and fitter in your body. The result is an epidemic of obesity on one side of the world and malnutrition and starvation on the other, and even those who are physically healthy are prone to tension, stress, fatigue, and depression, all of which are symptoms of low life force energy.

The problem is that we are focusing only on the calorific value of food whereas the energy of food goes beyond that. Calories provide the fuel for the physical body but the life force energy of food focuses on the mental and emotional bodies.

In this chapter you will learn that it is not only what you eat, but also how you have processed it and more importantly how you are eating matters and affects the life force energy of the food you are consuming. This eventually gets transformed and affects your life force energy. So if you constantly feel lazy and dull or extra charged and extra energized with certain emotions such as power or anger or control then it is a sign of the particular type of food derived life force energy you are adding more into your life. And it is this type of life force energy that attracts into your mind a certain type of thoughts pattern and certain types of emotions. And you think you are thinking them when in reality it's the life force energy of the food that you are eating that is making you who you are in terms of your thoughts and emotions.

Calorie VS Life Force Energy of Food

Food is energy and a proper diet provides correct type of fuel to sustain the energy of the individual consuming it. The underlying fact is that the body gets the energy that it needs to grow and maintain itself from air, water, and food, and, most importantly Prana (Life force energy).

According to Yoga and other holistic traditions food not only provides you with the energy to live as the physical fuel for the cells but also with the subtle aspect of the energy that supports our lives. Physical aspect of energy from the food we eat suggests that it is burnt in the digestive tract and then supplied to various organs and cells to provide energy for their metabolism. The life force view of the food suggests that you become what you eat not just physically but mentally as well. The type of food you eat influences your mind and its state. In fact it is not just the food that you eat that makes a difference but how we eat it and how the food was handled and prepared.

Lord Krishna says to Arjuna: "The food which is dear to each is threefold. Hear the distinctions of these. The foods which increase vitality, energy, vigour, health and joy, and which are delicious, bland, substantial and agreeable are dear to the pure. The passionate desire foods are those that are bitter, sour, saline, excessively hot, pungent, dry, and burning and which produce pain, grief and disease. The food which is stale, tasteless, putrid and rotten, leavings and impure is dear to the Tamasic." (Bhagavad-Gita. Ch. VII-8, 9, 10).

Ancient philosophy of Yoga categorises the food in 3 categories from a life force energy perspective: -

Tamasic: Tamasic food is the one that has negative life force energy. Tamas means dark and dull. A Tamasic diet doesn't benefit either the mind or the body because the Prana or life force energy is very little in it. It makes the mind dull, clouds the power of reasoning and sets in heaviness or inertia making you feel lazy, lethargic, and slow. It fills the mind filled with negative emotions, such as anger, jealousy, and greed. Body's resistance to diseases also gets reduced with such diet. Tamasic foods include meat, alcohol, tobacco, onions, garlic, fermented foods such as vinegar and stale left over food, contaminated or overripe substances, poultry, fish, eggs, alcohol, and other intoxicants including drugs. Foods that are over-processed and stale and difficult to digest are Tamasic. Foods that are prepared without consciousness or when the preparer is angry or in negative mood are also considered Tamasic. If you are interested in vital health and more positive energy in your life it is best to avoid these foods. In fact, overeating or stuffing the stomach with too much food is also regarded as Tamasic as it destroys the body's ability to absorb the life force energy from food along with the physical nutrients. Tamasic is the unhealthiest food.

Rajasic: Rajasic food has neutral Life force energy. Rajas signify passion and excitement creating energy. It is the energy, which we need to accomplish, create, and achieve. It represents worldly power and the drive to conquer and achieve. A Rajasic diet is good for people who aspire to maintain a peaceful meditative mind but still achieve well in the world as well. Foods that are very hot, bitter, sour, dry, or salty are Rajasic.

Rajasic foods include hot substances, such as sharp spices or strong herbs, stimulants, like coffee and tea, meat of animals and fish, eggs, salt and chocolate. Many of the under-ground foods are also Rajasic. Too much Rajasic food over stimulates the body and mind. It excites strong emotional qualities and passions making the mind restless and uncontrollable. If you eat your food in hurry then that also makes the food Rajasic even though it might be sattavic food in terms of contents that you are consuming. The emotion of hurry transforms the energetic quality of the food into Rajasic.

Sattavic: Positive Pranic energy food. Sattavic means pure essence. This is the purest diet for a consciously spiritual and healthy life. It nourishes the mind and body, and, maintains it in a peaceful state. According to Ayurveda, this is the best diet for physical strength, a good mind, good health, and longevity. It calms and purifies the mind, enabling it to function at its maximum potential. A Sattavic diet thus leads to true health - a peaceful mind in control of a fit body, with a balanced flow of energy between them. A Sattavic diet is excellent if you desire to live a quiet, peaceful and meditative life full of positive life force energy. These foods are supposed to produce calmness, peace, and compassion. The Sattavic diet consists of light, soothing, easily digestible food. Sattvic signifies the etheric qualities and includes foods such as fruits and vegetables, especially sun foods and ground foods. Many Sattvic foods are sun foods are those that grow one meter or more above the ground. They have a catalyzing and lightening effect on the body's nervous and digestive systems.

Ground foods are those foods that grow within one meter of the ground. They draw energy from the earth and are high in nutrients. Sattvic foods include sprouted whole grains, fresh fruit, land and sea vegetables, pure fruit juices, nut and seed milk, cheese, legumes, nuts, seeds, sprouted seeds, honey, and herbal tea. Sattvic foods are those which do not agitate your stomach at all. Simple, natural, non-stimulating, tissue-building, energy-producing, non-alcoholic food and drink keep the mind calm and pure.

Interestingly a French engineer Andre Simoneton developed a similar view of food. He divided foods into four general classes on the basis of the electromagnetic waves that they emitted. He used a scale of zero to 10,000 angstroms and he found the basic human wavelength to be about 6500. Foods that emit vibrations or wavelengths that match the human wavelength scale are considered best for our consumption.

According to his scientific research he classified the food as: -

First class of food: These are food such as fruits, fresh vegetables, whole grains, and so on which have the wavelength matching the human wavelength and more i.e. 6500 – 10,000. These foods if consumed would add to the energy of the person consuming it as it has more energy than its consumer.

Second class of food: These are food items with wavelength ranging from 6500 to 3,000 angstroms include eggs, peanut oil, wine, boiled vegetables, cane sugar, and cooked fish. Such food of course does not contribute much to the life force energy of its takers since they are vibrating at a frequency lower than the human wavelength.

Third category of food is with very weak wavelength falling below 3,000 angstroms include cooked meat, sausages, coffee, tea, chocolate, jams, processed cheese, and white bread.

Fourth category of food is that which exhibits practically no life force and is therefore practically dead. This includes margarine, alcoholic spirit, refined white sugar, and bleached flour.

Food processing takes the life force energy out of many foods and makes them heavy, dull, and lifeless or simply dead. All processed and refined foods lack Prana or life force energy. This includes white sugar, flour, and most types of breads, cheeses and cereals. The vital life force of these foods gets lost in their processing. That is why natural foods are always recommended. In fact items stored in tin cans, frozen foods, and pre-cooked meals, which have to be re-heated, are all severely deficient in life force energy and not recommended at all for positive life force energy aligned lifestyle. Such Prana-less foods have a tendency to weigh down the person consuming them, can clog up the digestive tract, and also promote the formation of bodily toxins and storage of excess fat.

Vegetables and fruits are high in Pranic content. And if you are wondering how to find out what is rich in Life force energy, then here are some tips: -

- The more vivid or vibrant the colour, the greater the life force energy contained in it, and also the higher its nutritional value. Of course this rule is not applicable if artificial methods are used to enhance the colour.

- Food that is fresh is rich in life force energy and tastes nice and has a more pleasing flavour. There is a difference in the taste of food, which has less life force often because the process of decay has already set in. It may taste more bitter or sour, depending on the food item.

- The aroma of foods rich in Prana pr life force energy is usually more vibrant and fresh whereas foods, which lack fragrance, smell bad or rancid are often with less life force energy in them.

Sun as the ultimate source of energy

All energy that we receive on this planet is from the SUN. Even the food that we eat essentially sources all the energy contained in it from the SUN. HOW? Well the answer is simple - all vegetarian food comes from plants. We all know that plants take their energy from the SUN and transforms it into food through photosynthesis and energy gets stored in the form of roots, stem, leaves, flowers and fruits. The entire body of the plant grows out of the process of transformation of the gross matter from soil and water into its body with the help of energy drawn from the SUN. Herbivorous animals then eat these plants to sustain themselves. The body of the herbivorous animals grows through eating the body of plants, which was assembled through the energy of the SUN; hence they too are taking the energy of SUN, though indirectly to survive. And then the completely carnivorous animals like lions and tigers eat these herbivorous animals thus acquiring the energy of the SUN contained in the body of herbivore from the plants. We as humans take our energy from our food either via plants or through cooked meat. Either way we are relying on SUN for our energy in the form of food.

How did you cook your food?

As stated earlier its not just what you eat is important but how it was cooked also matters and makes a huge difference in the quality of the life force energy derived from the food. The vibration of the individual who is preparing the food is also important. This aspect is however often neglected when the quality of the nourishment from food is considered. If the person doing the cooking is full of worries, anger or negativity, then these vibrations get transferred into the meal. Although the effects would be quite subtle initially, however their cumulative effects can be serious, particularly if you are continuously exposed to food with such negative energy.

If the person who is cooking your food is short tempered, it is recommended that you either cook the meal yourself or make some other arrangements. Intense emotional vibrations permeate the food and affect your mind eventually. You might get the physical nutrition but you will also intake the emotions with which the food was cooked. It is not recommended that you don't eat food cooked by someone who is sick or emotionally disturbed, suffering from pain or any other kind of negativity. Even in restaurants, if the staff cooking the food is not well treated or is underpaid you can imagine what will go into your mind along with the food that you eat there.

On the other hand if someone prepares a meal with love and affection, these vibrations will also get transmitted into the food. It will be satisfying beyond merely the physical aspects of taste and nutrition. No wonder why we cannot forget the food we ate as a child cooked by our mother or grandmother. The love vibration in that food cannot match any restaurant any master-chef's cooked food. Isn't that true?

Personally in my house I play a mantra, which generates positive vibrations in the kitchen while cooking. This greatly influences the mind of the person cooking in the kitchen, which is usually my wife and me, and also the sound energy of the mantra enhances the life force energy of the food directly.

Any item, which has been refrigerated for a long period of time, also loses much of its life force energy content, and the same is applicable to over cooked food. Over cooked food would usually imply that the life force energy has been drained out of it almost entirely along with much of the nutrients. Therefore, vegetables should be cooked lightly, so that their vibrancy is maintained. You can boil the life out of your vegetables and eat dead food if you want. A steamer is a nice addition to a kitchen, or even a pressure cooker, as long as the food is not over cooked. Besides duration of cooking, leftover food also become life force deficient, simply because it has been re-refrigerated or re-heated to the point where their vitality is completely gone. Cooked food if eaten after a significant lapse also looses much of its life force.

Eat Intuitively

As we work with more life force energy we understand and appreciate the value of intuition in making choices and decisions. You can use your intuition to identify the type of food that suits your body the most. Eat intuitively, which simply means "Eat when you're hungry and stop when you're full". Listen for the body's signals that tell you that you are no longer hungry. Observe the signs that show that you're comfortably full.

Pause in the middle of a meal and check with yourself how the food tastes, and how full you are? Trust yourself with your own readings of body signals in terms of what food to eat, how much to eat, when to eat, and gradually your choices will start aligning with what is best for you and suits you the most. Rather than relying on prescriptions of food diet simply follow your body's signals and make choices in line with it.

When you eat what you really want, in a suitably conducive environment the food will taste much nicer and the pleasure you derive will make you feel satisfied and contented. You will find that it takes not much food to satisfy both your stomach and the taste buds. You will start making food choices that honor your health and taste buds and also make you feel well. You will realize that you don't have to eat a perfect diet to be healthy. Just as a person with a shoe size of eight cannot expect to realistically squeeze into size six, it is equally as futile (and uncomfortable) to have the same expectations from body size. On certain days you might need a lunch full of potatoes, rice, and curry. On some other day, the craving may be just be for salad. Sometimes you might want to have heavy breakfast just because you were that hungry. On other days, light dinner could be more than enough.

Mindful Eating Vs Mouthful eating

Eat mindfully and not like a zombie stuffing your stomach with something and anything without being aware only to find out the next day what you actually ate ☺ Here are some tips on how to eat your food for maximum life force energy intake and assimilation:

- Smell, touch, and taste each bite. You should eat with all the five senses getting involved. See your food and admire it, smell it, touch to feel its texture, and then taste it feeling full taste with each bite.

- Avoid eating in standing posture or while walking.

- Eat in a clean pretty plate and in clean surroundings. This will automatically simulate your digestive juices and prepare your body and mind to get ready.

- Eat slowly, chewing your food as much as you can. There is a saying eat liquid food as slowly as if it is solid and eat solid food by chewing it so much such that it becomes liquid.

- Take small sips of water between bites, this helps the digestion and also helps reducing the intake by filling the stomach with water. However water should not be in large quantities. Just o sip, else the water will interfere with the digestion.

- Take a deep breath before eating. This energises your mind, increases the flow of blood in your body, particularly the digestive track.

- Eat your favourite food last. This helps reducing cravings and also keeps your mouth enjoy the type of taste you admire the most for a longer time leaving you with more satisfaction.

- Eat food that is good for you first, that leaves less room in your mind and the stomach for the less nourishing food. I learnt this from my gym instructor who suggested me to first eat a full plate of salad and then satisfy rest of the hunger with bread, lentils, curry, and so on.

- Eat food with a feeling of gratitude, so that it gets absorbed completely in your body providing necessary nourishment.

How much to Eat

According to yoga and ayurveda, the size of human stomach is the same as the size of the fist. So if you make your fist it closely resembles the size of your stomach. This gives an idea on how much food you can eat to be stomach full. However it doesn't stay there. For optimum health and digestion it is recommended that only half the stomach be filled with food one fourth with water and one fourth left empty for air for easy digestion. This goes hand in hand with mindful eating rather than listening to the call of our stomach and the tongue, which is fine. You should eat tasty food and enjoy it completely. If the food doesn't feel good to the senses the body will completely reject it irrespective of any amount of nutrition it has. So an important issue is how to regulate the amount that we eat and yet satisfy our taste buds completely. The answer lies in effort to extract maximum taste from each bite that you take. Rather than gulping your food straight into your guts and then trying to eat more and more to satisfy your taste buds chew your bite as much as you can. It will have an additional benefit as the more you chew the better it will mix with saliva starting the digestion process straight in the mouth.

Blessing the Food increases its Life force Energy

It is strange how the world of energy works, but yes prayers and blessings while taking the food do increase the life force energy of the food significantly. It could be as simple as blessing your food with your own love and affection and have a feeling of gratitude that it is supporting your life and nourishing you. You might think how would the vitamins and minerals get affected by blessing the food, and how can it make a difference. Simple answer is" try it". Try to eat your food after blessing it and then some day try eating the same food with a negative emotion and you will feel the difference yourself.

Chapter 2:
Energy From Breath

Do you want to experience tranquility and peace through out the day without doing any meditation?

Do you want to learn how you can revitalize your body, your energy levels, and your mind by simply controlling your breath?

Life Force Energy

It's crazy but let me tell you that you are messing up something that you do almost 25,000 times everyday. Yes its true - it's inhaling and exhaling, that is your breathing. Most of us are not aware of how to properly and efficiently do such a simple yet life-generating activity like breathing. And it is not just how to gulp in more air but it's a complete science, which can regulate and revitalize your body, your mind and emotions, and enhance your complete energy levels. Most people however suck in the bare minimum air with each inhalation underutilizing the full capacity of their lungs and depriving their body of the right amount of oxygen it should receive. And it is not just oxygen that we are inhaling but also the life force energy the Prana that we intake with each and every breath. So breathing serves two functions, firstly, providing the oxygen for the body and secondly, exchanging the vital life force energy with the universe. Lower levels of life force energy make you prone to illness, morbid emotions, and, weak physical and mental performance. Also when done properly breathing facilitates higher oxygen intake. It also balances the oxygen-carbon dioxide exchange in the body, which empowers your metabolism.

Science of breathing

Interestingly enough if you realise breathing is the only process that you can do both voluntarily and involuntarily. You can breathe unconsciously as you do most of the time, in which case the breathing happens in the background as an involuntary function like beating of heart. You can also breathe consciously bringing it under your control, where in you can breathe fast or slow, or can even stop breathing for a while (you can't do this with your heart beat, though ☺). If you are breathing unconsciously then you transfer control to the primitive parts of the brain where subconscious emotions, thoughts and feelings influence you, with you having no direct awareness but only passive response to them. However, once you start breathing consciously with awareness the frontal part of the brain, which is the more advanced and evolved, registers, the breath and becomes activated allowing you to have conscious control on your thoughts, feelings, and emotions. Incorrect or irregular breathing often triggers various disturbances in the body and mind.

Quick and shallow breathing promotes ageing factors and is detrimental to your physical and emotional well-being. Deep Yogic breathing has proved to release endorphins in the bloodstream which are important chemicals in the brain that helps in relaxing the brain and help in eliminating fear, anxiety, and pain. A 2011 study found that just one 20-minute session of yogic breathing increases the flow of oxygenated blood to your brain, enhances activity in the prefrontal cortex, the area associated with ability of concentration. Yogic breathing also raises levels of the serotonin also called the happy hormone, which uplifts your mood and can help release stress and depression.

Life force energy of Breath

So what is the link between Prana and air, life force energy and oxygen, are they the same thing? When we are breathing we are exchanging both air, which consists of oxygen and also Prana, which is the life force energy that sustains us. Both life force energy and oxygen are like twin siblings in that they are both vital for our existence but are not the same. And this is proven by the yogis who prefer to meditate on high mountaintops where the oxygen is quite low but Prana is quite abundant. They choose to meditate high up on mountaintops to tap the vast life force energy present there and there the reliance is less on oxygen for survival.

The most obvious manifestation of life force energy in the human body is the motion of lungs. If that stops, all other manifestations of the life force in body will come to an end. So Prana or life force energy is not what the lungs are inhaling and exhaling but it is what is causing the lungs to inhale and exhale.

Breath and Mind

If you study your breathing patterns you will become aware of the how your moods and emotions change. Long and deep breathing helps you create and stabilize a strong, steady breathing pattern that will mitigate excessive emotional swings. It retrains your nervous system to relax and makes your thoughts more positive and comfortable. Shallow breathing makes people prone to lung weaknesses in the face of environmental problems, such as polluted air and can also lead to depression. Fear tends to produce erratic, strained, or weak breathing patterns.

Breath and mind are closely linked. In fact the only way you can control your thoughts consistently and influence our mind is through the breath. This is discussed further in Chapter 6 - Thoughts as Energy. Basically thoughts are very subtle manifestations of life force energy and cannot be controlled directly. Here is a simple yet powerful story that explains this clearly.

There was a princess that was caught and locked at the top of a tower with no access to it. The prince came to rescue her but was not sure how to get up there and how to climb the tower. He saw ants climbing up the tower. He had a rope but that was too heavy for the ants to carry up. Then an idea struck him, he tied a small thread to one of the ants. As the ant went up the light small thread also went up with it. The princess picked the thread up through the window of the top chamber of tower. Then the prince standing on the ground picked another thread that was slightly heavier than the earlier one but not too heavy. He tied this heavier thread to the thread the other end of which the princess was now holding. And the princess slowly pulled up the bigger, heavier and stronger thread. Now again the Prince repeated the same thing, hanging a slightly stronger thread each time and asking the Princess to pull up the more stronger thread with the help of the lesser one. Soon he was able to send the strong rope up to the Princess using which she could come down and be rescued. So the moral of the story is that just like the Prince could not send the rope straight away to the Princess he had to use the lighter threads first similarly we can control the big jolts of thoughts directly by our physical will. However we can control our breath through our physical will. This breath is like that small starting thread that will eventually enable the heavy rope of mind to be pulled. But you have to start gradually with your breath.

Through your breath you can conquer your mind. That is why Yoga lays so much emphasis on breathing and the importance of deep regulated breathing.

Besides the energetic aspect of the breathing that we shared in earlier chapter this is the other aspect of breath in terms of its linkage to the mind, to the thoughts coming in the mind. If you observe your selves or others closely you can see matching patterns between your breath and thinking. The shallower the breath the more dispersed the mind, full of thoughts running around like loose canons in a battlefield. The deeper the breath you take the smaller the number of thoughts. And this is visible even otherwise when you experience certain emotional states such as anger, the thoughts triggered generate a response of fast and shallow breathing. At that moment when you are angry if you focus on your breath and make it slow and deep you can immediately feel that your emotions of anger will subside.

Yogic Breathing

So you see as you exert more control on your breathing you start to exert control over your finer mental processes and thought patterns. Conscious breathing with awareness and using the right techniques contribute immensely to how much life force energy you can exchange, imbibe, and reserve in your body. The focus of yogic breathing is not just healthy exchange of oxygen but also on relaxing the overall nervous system and most importantly work on the exchange on Prana or the Life Force Energy.

Yogic breathing divides the breath into 3 stages: -

- Inhalation or Purak
- Kumbhak or the pause between the inhalation and exhalation
- Rechak or exhalation.

A simple rule suggested for effective life force breathing is to have a ratio of 1:2 between inhalation and exhalation, or simply the length of your exhalation should be twice the length of your inhalation. This is the secret to Yogic Breathing; fuller exhalations double the length of inhalation. This helps get rid of the carbon dioxide and also frees up extra space for better and deeper inhalation. In more advanced practices the ratio is 1:2:4 between Inhalation, holding, and exhalation. Longer exhalation also signals the nervous system to slow down and lowers your heart rate relaxing you still further. To start with, even if you focus on balancing the inhalation and exhalation making them equal in duration will get good results.

Here are some easy to do exercises to improve your breathing and align it with life force rich yogic breathing. The first step of life force rich yogic breathing is to become aware of your breathing process. This is very simple:

- Sit comfortably with your spine straight or lie down and relax your body completely.

- Now just become aware of the breathing pattern. Do not try to change or control the pattern, just witness the natural inhalation and exhalation.

- Do not modify or control the breath in any way just observe as a silent witness.

- Become aware of the primordial mantra SO-HUM with your breath. Every inhalation makes the sound SO, and every exhalation sounds like HUM. Become aware of this mantra with every inhalation and exhalation and this will deepen your connection with the breath.

- Awareness of each breath makes you relax deeper and slowly you will find that you are only aware of your breath and not your body. The body will cease to exist and only the breath will be there to be felt. This will bring complete relaxation and rejuvenation of your body and mind.

- Now slowly start coming back into the body by becoming more aware of the body and less aware of your breath, slowly moving your fingers and hands.

Then the next step is to breath in a measured way in and out. This will harmonize the system. You can use a clock to measure or a better way is to add a mantra to the breathing so for example use the mantra OM. Inhale counting Om five times and then exhale counting the same mantra Om five times. Let the word flow in and out with your breath rhythmically and you will feel that your entire body is becoming relaxed and rhythmical.

Full Yogic Breath for complete Life Force Energy:

The lungs have three lobes or chambers and most people use only the middle lobe for breathing. The upper and lower lobes are not completely used. Full yogic breathing helps in activating and utilizing the entire capacity of lungs. The following exercise helps you rediscover the natural process of breathing. If you watch baby's breath, they would be breathing in this way with their abdomen expanding first and then their chest. Here are the steps: -

- Lie down comfortably and relax your body completely.

- Inhale slowly and deeply filling in your lower lungs completely with air expanding your abdomen.

- Keep breathing in and now feel the air filling your middle part of lungs and expanding your thoracic cavity or chest.

- Now you would be almost full with breath however inhale a little more filling the upper lobes of the lungs pushing the shoulders and collar bones slightly up.

- Now start exhaling emptying the upper lobes of lungs first relaxing the collarbones and shoulders.

- Then as a continuous process relax the chest exhaling from the lungs.

- Finally releasing the air starching your abdomen.

- Try to empty the lungs as much as you can without straining them.

- This completes one round. Try doing this for up to 10 breaths to start with.

Affect of breath on posture: If you are breathing correctly then you cannot maintain a bad posture for your spine. Try practicing full yogic breath with drooping shoulders or a curved spine. It won't happen. That's the beauty of the human body. Good posture leads to good breath leading to relaxed nerves and increased life force energy. The three parts of the body the chest, neck, and the head should be held in a straight line and free the thoracic cavity, diaphragm and the abdomen to inhale and exhale freely.

Benefits of Yogic Breathing

- Increases oxygen intake.

- Releases accumulated carbon dioxide and the toxic waste products build up in the blood, to be released through prolonged exhalation.

- Increases mental capacities and clarity and releases stress in the body.

- Retrains your nervous system to relax.

- Deep yogic breathing methods transfer the pressure from air coming into the lungs to the internal organs, especially the heart. This provides a gentle yet firm massage for the organs while increasing blood and life force energy flow that helps to optimize their natural range of movement. This improves the functioning of your internal organs.

- Increases the life force energy reserves in the body. You will feel more energy at your disposal; ability to recover from unexpected unwanted situations will be easier. You can maintain a steady positive state of mind and body easily.

The two nostrils, yin and yang and the two hemispheres of brain

The two nostrils are linked to the two main nadis in the energy body Ida and Pingala. When we breathe with one nostril we energise one particular Nadi, but first a little introduction to the energy body.

According to yogic and other holistic sciences we all have an energy body. The energy body is an exact replica of the physical body. This Energy body or Prana Sharir in the Yogic texts is an invisible energy system facilitating flow of life force energy through pathways or energy meridians called Nadis. These meridians have multiple pressure points that serve as means of working on the energy to keep it flowing and moving. Acupressure, acupuncture, and reflexology are some common modalities for manipulating energy flows by acting on the pressure points. The Nadis are the astral tubes made of astral matter, and serve as passages for life force energy to flow through and operate in the subtle energy body, very much like the nerves, arteries and veins in the gross physical body. Of millions of nadis that the energy body has, there are three main ones

Sushumna Nadi: This is the central vertical channel that goes from root chakra* (explained in the next chapter) right up to the Sahasrar chakra* at the top of the head and beyond.
Ida Nadi: Starting from the Root Chakra, on the right side of the spinal column, the Ida extends spirally around the Sushumna Nadi and extends up to the left nostril.

Pingala Nadi: Starting from the same chakra on the left side of the spinal column, the Pingala extends spirally up to the right nostril.

From here the Ida and Pingala Nadis meet and coil up spirally and terminate in between the two eyebrows forming The Third Eye or the 6th Chakra.

Breathing through Left Nostril: The left nostril activates Ida Nadi. If you breathe through the left nostril then you are energizing the life force energy with negative charge or feminine energy. Ida is the channel for lunar or cold energy. If you breathe only through Ida you will promote a receptive, emotional, and compassionate energy.

Breathing through Right Nostril: Pingala Nadi is activated by breathing through the right nostril. This imparts a positive charge to the life force energy and makes it more masculine in nature. Pingala is the channel for solar or hot energy. If you breathe only through Pingala you will promote a more action oriented, mental, and dynamic energy.

Breathing through mouth: If you breathe through your mouth rather than through the nostrils you will not get the negative and positive life force energy. This will result in your becoming lethargic and sick.

Breathing simultaneously through left and right nostrils equalizes the use of the right and left hemispheres of the brain. Wouldn't it be wonderful to have this balance? This is the door to true success, ability to think both creatively and logically and becoming a genius. Would you like to learn how to achieve this balance and change your life by changing your thinking pattern? Here is a practice called as Anulom Vilom that will help you achieve this.

This is also called alternate nostril breathing as is very powerful in balancing the right and left hemispheres of the brain. Below steps provide instruction on one complete round of Anulom Vilom breathing. Start by practicing three to five rounds and then slowly build the practice up to twenty.

- Breathe in through the left nostril, closing the right with the thumb. Count till four.

- Hold the breath closing both nostrils to the count of six or eight.

- Breath out through the right nostril now closing the left with ring and little fingers to the count of eight.

- Breath in through the right nostril keeping the left nostril closed with the ring and little fingers to the count of four.

- Again hold the breath to the count of six or eight as comfortable.

- Breath out through the left nostril keeping right closed with the thumb to the count of eight.

- Repeat the above steps to continue the cycle.

Life Force Energy

Chapter 3:
Energy From Chakras

Do you want to achieve best of health and experience absolute happiness all the time?

Do you want to experience 7 times more energy than you currently have by unblocking the 7 powerhouses of energy within you?

Life Force Energy

Your body has hundreds of energy centers within them for tempering, controlling, pushing, transmitting and receiving energy from inside-outside, and vice versa. However, there are seven key energy centers within us – governing particular parts of our physical body and various emotional and spiritual attributes as well, widely known as the chakras. These chakras ('wheels' or 'vortexes' in English) are powerful, pulsating centers of energy, which are located in a straight line running through the center of our body along the spine. The first one is located at the tip of our tailbone, and the last seventh one lies at the top of our head. These chakras connect us both to the earth below us and the heavens above, and, inspire us in equal measure.

Each chakra is responsible for not only providing our bodies with the energy it requires in order to function happily and healthily, but also to ensure that our emotional lives move in a positive direction and our connection with the divine is felt and understood, that our true voices and inspiration get discovered and utilized, and path in life can be chosen and followed freely and creatively.

When the root, sacral, solar plexus, heart, throat, third eye, and crown chakras open and spin, as they should, we live happy, confident, and liberated lives. They allow us to work, nurture, express ourselves and love one another, as well as, make us feel special and unique and loved by others.

As such, it is vitally important not merely for your physical health but also for our all-round and holistic health that your chakras are well looked after and remain open and unblocked. In case certain chakra or chakras become blocked or get depleted of energy, various symptoms of this blockage start manifesting themselves in your life. Depending on which chakra is affected, this could be anything from physical health problems to loss of confidence or faith in oneself, indecisiveness, a loss of passion or sensuality, or overpowering feeling of loneliness or loss in faith.

More knowledge on chakras will help you in discovering how they are related to emotions and influence them. Apart from it, you can even see how the legacy of your family shapes your present feelings, beliefs, and thoughts. You can also discover how they directly affect the present state of health of your organs and tissues.

There are seven chakras or energy vortexes in your body. These chakras help you to live happily and successfully. If the seven chakras are open and well-balanced, success will never be impossible for you to achieve at all times.

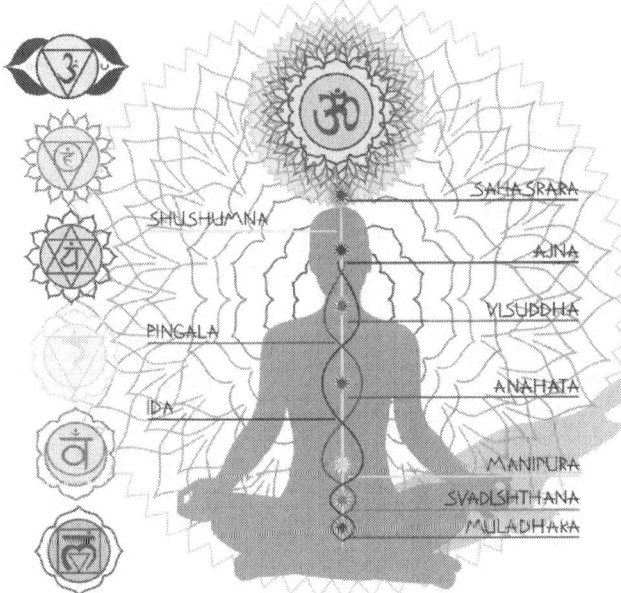

The 7 Chakras and their Location

Every major chakra can be found on the front of your body and it is being paired with its counterpart on the back of your body. Together they are being recognized to be the rear and front sides of the chakra. The rear aspects are related to a person's will and the frontal aspect is related to the person's feelings.

Each chakra is vibration of energy. The higher the chakra is located along the spine the higher is its frequency range. Thus we see that the chakras start from the root level in red color followed by chakras in orange, yellow, green, blue, indigo and violet colors, representing the seven colors of rainbow converging into violet at the top.

The first chakra has lessons that related to the material world. The second chakra provides us with lessons that are related to physical desire, work, and sexuality. The third chakra has lessons related to self-esteem, personality, and ego. The fourth chakra has cues related to compassion, forgiveness, and love. The fifth chakra provides us with lessons that are related to self-expression and will. The sixth chakra has lessons related to wisdom, insight, intuition, and mind. The seventh chakra provides us with lessons related to spirituality.

Even if you believe or do not believe in chakras as literal places inside the body, they can still help you in activating body and mind connections for your total and complete health and healing.

When your energy is leaking, weak, or frozen you will feel depleted, heavy and even stuck! When you are energy-depleted and challenged, it is quite difficult to manage your emotions, have positive thoughts, stay healthy and attract harmony in your life.

You will feel the following effects as a result of Chakra Awakening and Chakra Balancing:

- Release of stuck emotions and negativity.
- A greater sense of joy, love and peace and living in the present moment.
- Empathy, Compassion and fulfilling relationships
- Intuitive decision making that may lead to substantial life changes.
- Transformations in career and relationships.
- Better physical health and recovery from illness.
- Living life in tune with your true self, experiencing more contentment.
- Breakthroughs on a personal level and personal transformation.

Anatomy of Chakras

The chakras can actually be visualized as lotus flowers of different colors with varying number of petals determining their functions and frequency of vibration at various locations in the body. The chakras regulate and give us huge amount of influence on our physical and mental being. Anatomically chakras can be described through the color they represent, the number of petals each has, the divine elemental energy they represent, esoteric symbols and much more. Some of these properties are described in general below and then subsequently in the chapter for each individual chakra.

Color: Each chakra is associated with certain color, which represents its state of vibration. Starting from the root level in red color and converging into violet at the top, the chakras represent seven colors of the rainbow.

Petals: The number of petals are as per the psycho-physical-emotional function that the chakra is supposed to support. For example, it is very interesting to see that Ajna Chakra has two petals to balance the left and the right brain and their representative logical and creative energies, or to see that Sahasrar Chakra has thousand petals representing infinity as it is responsible for our connection to the infinite consciousness.

Element: The seven chakras represent the seven elements of the Universe from gross to subtle from bottom to top. Starting with Mooladhar which represents the Earth element which is all about grounding, security, and safety, to Water element represented by the Swadhisthan Chakra to Fire representing courage by the Manipura Chakra, and so on.

Symbol: Each chakra has an esoteric symbol within it, for example Heart chakra has symbol Star of David representing the union of Male and Female energies through the intersection of upward and downward triangles, symbolizing harmony and love.

Location: As already mentioned the locations of various chakras correspond largely to the endocrine glands the corresponding chakra supports.

Beej Mantra: This is the seed sound of the chakra. Just like color has a visual energetic representation of the chakra similarly this is a representation of the element of the chakra in the form of sound vibrations.

Endocrine Gland: The chakras influence the body largely through the endocrine system. Each chakra regulates a particular endocrine gland. For example, the Ajna Chakra regulates the master Pituitary gland and the Sahasrar Chakra regulates the Pineal gland, which is calcified or dormant in most of us.

Associated Organs: Each chakra energizes a particular set of physical organs in our body. This association is not linear but largely influenced by the chakras located near or around that organ and its other emotional and physical influences.

Emotional Blockage: This is a very strong connection that the chakras have over our well being. As stated in a previous chapter chakras influence our emotional states and a particular type of chakra is responsible for a certain type of emotional experience in its healthy, balanced or dysfunctional form.

Life Lesson: Chakras represent our evolution in life from the lower selfish, survival related state to the state of achievement, love, self-expression, intuition, and unity. Each chakra functions so that we can experience and draw a particular life ranging from human selfishness to divine selflessness.

Mooladhar Chakra

Chakra Property	Description	Chakra Property	Description
Color	Red	Petals	4
Element	Earth	Symbol	Square
Location	Perineum, between Anus and Genitals	Beej Mantra:	Lam
Endocrine Gland	Adrenals	Associated Organs	Bones, kidneys, spinal column, colon,
Emotional blockages	Safety, Security	Life Lesson	Standing up for one self, Survival, Physical needs

Chapter 3 : Energy From Chakras

Swadhisthan Chakra

Chakra Property	Description	Chakra Property	Description
Color	Orange	Petals	6
Element	Water	Symbol	Upturned crescent moon
Location	About 2 inches below naval	Beej Mantra:	Vam
Endocrine Gland	Genitals-Ovaries, Testes	Associated Organs	Sex organs, prostate, womb
Emotional blockages	Guilt, Shame	Life Lesson	Emotional balance, sexuality

Manipura Chakra

Chakra Property	Description	Chakra Property	Description
Color	Yellow	Petals	10
Element	Fire	Symbol	Inverted or descending triangle
Location	Naval	Beej Mantra:	Ram
Endocrine Gland	Pancreas	Associated Organs	Digestive system, muscles
Emotional blockages	Fear, Anger	Life Lesson	Power, Self will, Self esteem, self confidence

Anahat Chakra

Chakra Property	Description	Chakra Property	Description
Color	Green	Petals	12
Element	Sky	Symbol	Start of David representing the union of Male and Female energy
Location	Centre of chest	Beej Mantra:	Yam
Endocrine Gland	Thymus	Associated Organs	Heart, chest, blood circulation
Emotional blockages	Sadness, Resentment, Hurt, melancholy	Life Lesson	Love and Relationships, Forgiveness and compassion

Vishuddhi Chakra

Chakra Property	Description	Chakra Property	Description
Color	Blue	Petals	16
Element	Space or Ether principle	Symbol	Circle within a descending triangle
Location	Base of neck	Beej Mantra:	Ham
Endocrine Gland	Thyroid	Associated Organs	Mouth, throat, ears
Emotional blockages	Suppression, Inability to express, blocked creativity	Life Lesson	Communication, Self expression, creative identity

Ajna Chakra

Chakra Property	Description	Chakra Property	Description
Color	Indigo	Petals	2
Element	Inner Guru or Mind principle	Symbol	Descending triangle within a circle
Location	Between the eye brows	Beej Mantra:	Om
Endocrine Gland	Pituitary	Associated Organs	Eyes, nose, lower brain, nervous system
Emotional blockages	Nightmares, learning difficulties	Life Lesson	Emotional intelligence, Intuition, wisdom

Sahasrar Chakra

Chakra Property	Description	Chakra Property	Description
Color	Violet	**Petals**	1000 representing infinite
Element	God principle,	**Symbol**	Thousand petal lotus
Location	Just above the crown of the head	**Beej Mantra:**	No Sound / Om
Endocrine Gland	Pineal	**Associated Organs**	Upper brain
Emotional blockages	Depression, self centeredness, spiritual poverty, chaos	**Life Lesson**	Spirituality, Selflessness

Please note colored Chakra Cards can be downloaded from my website: www.LifeForceEnergyBook.com

Chapter 4:
Thoughts as Energy

Do you ever say to your self 'I must not forget that' and then go and forget it or 'don't spill the spaghetti on your shirt' and you know what happens next?

Do you want to be able to harness the most powerful instrument available to you for creating your reality?

Thoughts are programs of energy that create a ripple in the cosmic mind set in motion creating physical results. Thoughts have power. In fact they constitute the most powerful instrument that is available to humans. Everything starts as a thought first and then moves into the physical dimension through the actions that you take to under their influence. All the inventions can be attributed to the power of thoughts reflecting the unique ability of humans to think, analyse, become aware, and take action. Think about something and you move towards it. And even if you are thinking about something that you don't want you sill still move towards it ☺. If I say to you, 'Don't think about the colour Green, the colour of grass, the leaves of the trees, don't think about it', what does this fill your mind with? GREEN COLOR Isn't it? ☺. That is why it is so important to be aware of your mental chatter to be able to control it. The chatter is consuming your energy and taking you in a direction in which you either want to go or don't want to go. Isn't that RIGHT?

Don't you agree with me? The limit of your thought is the limit of the possibilities. Your circumstances and environment are the materialisation of your thoughts. The world experience varies in accordance with your thoughts. Whatever thought is cherished by you will be ultimately realised. All your states of happiness or misery are effects of your own thoughts. Your present state is willed by your thoughts. You can change your present state by changing your present thoughts. The world around you is only what you believe it to be. Your perceptions are coloured by your thoughts. The mind perceives and continues to perceive the things in that very form in which it imagines it to be with full faith.

Haphazard thinking = Loss of energy

Have you ever experienced fatigue or tiredness after an intense session of mental activity? How do you feel after a class of mathematics or physics, or an intense analytical discussion in which you sat on a chair and probably only moved your fingers and your head? TIRED isn't it? Don't you feel that the session drained your energy? This simply tells that THINKING CONSUMES ENERGY. Although thoughts do not appear as physical entities yet it requires energy in order to think. If we look at it the other way round, if you are starving or are tired in the evening after a hectic day you find it difficult to think, to concentrate, you just want to relax, shut your eyes, take a nap or do something that requires less mental activity. You need to rejuvenate your mind with energy in order to be back again functioning in a lively and more structured way.

So you can now see the important link between thoughts and energy. And most of the time you are spending your valuable energy simply thinking something or the other not even aware of what you are thinking. Of course you need to think, but you need to spend your energy wisely. Thinking in a structured way, when you are required to think, to solve a problem, to analyse a situation that will add value to someone, to you, in your job, at your home in your business etc.

How I created thought control

Let me share with you my story about how I cultured thought control. This happened when I was in the third year of my engineering studies. As always, I was quite passionate about yoga and specially its effect on mind. So I decided to test the effects of some of the breathing exercises, particularly Anulom Vilom or alternate nostril breathing. I practiced it along with some other meditation every day two times a day for 30 minutes. It helped quieten my mind considerably but I was in for a shock soon. After around a month or so my semester end exams started. The exam on thermo dynamics one of the most difficult subjects in engineering was round the corner when one of my friends called me. He asked me if I had completed a particular chapter. Now I don't remember the name of the chapter but it was definitely a tough one. I asked him if he has and how much time did it take him to do so, so that I could plan my preparation. He told me it took him around 6 hours to understand and complete it. I put down the phone, and asked myself how much time I will take to complete it after practicing all these breathing and meditation techniques. I started and to my surprise I could finish it in just less than two hours. I was amazed - the difference was in my awareness.

Earlier, when I used to study I would study for 5-10 minutes and then my mind would start wandering for and I could realise that my mind had gone off the subject. Well now as soon as my mind was about to drift I was aware of it and could bring it back. I could see it for myself now that one could achieve so much efficiency and sharpness through these practices. Isn't this amazing? To become aware of the movement of your thoughts in your mind and be able to control them.

Chapter 4 : Thoughts as Energy

Creating reality with thoughts

Everything is created twice, first in the mind through imagination and then in the physical reality through words and action. Thoughts precede words and action. You first think of the word or the action in your mind and then execute it through speech and/or action. The words we speak and the actions we take create our reality and results. That is why there is so much emphasis on positive thinking as positive thoughts will lead to positive words and positive action, which in turn will lead to positive results. But is it possible to think positively just by reading about positive thinking? I guess no. Otherwise, I might not have been writing this book as there would have been no readers as everyone would have already been positive, energetic and successful or at least the whole psychosomatic disease industry would have been out of business. Thought is energy. Your thought creates your environment. `Your thought constitutes your world. If you entertain good thoughts you can keep good health but on the other hand if you hold on to sickly thoughts you can never expect good health, beauty, and harmony in your life. Remember that the body is the product of the mind and is under the control of the mind. Thoughts of love peace, contentment, and purity will make you and also those around you more peaceful, happy, and contented.

Continue to dwell on what you want and you will achieve it. We attract in our life what we think about the most. By disciplining your thoughts you determine what you achieve. We should strive for thoughts that make us feel happy instead of sad, thoughts that bring us wealth instead of poverty, and thoughts that bring you health instead of disease.

Mental Rehearsal: Energy of thought has the capability to change the structure of our brain. Repeated thinking can create new neuro-pathways. This concept is now utilised in sports training. The athletes are asked to imagine in their minds their practice session. There has been scientifically published research acknowledging improvements in the performance of athletes through mental rehearsal of their sport. To learn anything or for improving it you require constant practice. The practice when done creates new neuro-pathways in the brain, which are responsible for the improvement in the performance. It is scientifically proven that the same neuro-pathways are created in the brain either if you practice physically or mentally. Thoughts are energy that has the power to affect your brain. You can improve your golf game, your public speaking, your driving skills, your confidence and any other ability you choose by using the energy of thoughts to re-pattern your brain.

Judgement and Quietening the mind: Considerable thinking is spent in judging people and circumstances. You are taught since childhood to analyse, think, evaluate, label things as right or wrong. It's almost a habit to do this on a day-to-day basis with anything and everything. Judging and labelling has become a game or rather a disease in itself.

If you could monitor your thoughts for a day and see what percentage of it gets utilised in what type of activity, you would find a considerably high percentage being utilised in judgment and labelling. It is important to evaluate things and make decisions. Most of the time people are busy judging and labelling things even when it is not required. One of the best way to cut our thought energy bills is to become less judgmental about the activities of other people, about what's going to happen if this happens or that happens. Such thinking has no constructive outcome but it does make your thought energy bills soar. The energy that you could have utilised in other fruitful activities such as learning a new sport or hobby, helping someone, doing some charity or completing a project that you have been holding on for long gets wasted. Too much thinking is overrated. It's an outcome of an education system that promotes intellectualism rather than pragmatism. Cutting through the clouds of thoughts brings you to the present moment and present is precisely the abode of peace and happiness. You can either be sad by bringing in thoughts of past and brooding over them or apprehensive by projecting thoughts on to a fearful future scenario. Either ways both the past and present are not real except while being part of your imagination. You are drawing in the energy of your past or future into your present moment through your thoughts.

You are not your thoughts

Most of your day is spent in thinking innumerable thoughts. Have you wondered from where these thoughts are coming? Are these your thoughts? I mean of course you are thinking these thoughts, so they are appearing in your mind, but who is creating them. Are you the one creating all these thoughts?

The answer is both yes and no. Probably 10% of these thoughts could be purely your own thoughts. In fact in today's super connected world we are bombarded with information through emails, social media, news channels, and so on it could be that you haven't had a single original thought that you can call your own throughout the day. So let's see what are the sources of our thoughts and from where do they appear in our mind: -

- **Collective mind:** This is interesting that although most people know about conscious and subconscious minds, few people are aware of the collective mind. All our minds are connected to a universal collective mind or thought matrix. Every thought we think creates a vibration in the collective mind and influences it. It gets stored in it energetically. That is why within so many cultures there are collective prayers that focus on sending thoughts of peace and happiness in the collective thought matrix to benefit all. Another interesting evidence of this is of the collective mind influencing the scientists for similar inventions at the same time, for example NYLON if you know the name comes from to cities New York and London, because it was simultaneously invented in both the cities without sharing any information on the physical level.

Another point to become aware of is that this collective thought field is dense with a particular types of thoughts at certain types of places and you can easily feel it. For example it is very difficult to feel peaceful in a shopping mall or in a stadium full of football fans. You get plugged in to the frequency of the collective thought field there, which is full of excitement, exuberance or chaos. An important thing to become aware of is that this collective thought field subconsciously or rather subtly influences you.

What you might think as your own thoughts most of the times are actually thoughts from the collective field influencing you. For example you might be inspired to follow your calling, your dream say to quit your job and start a business to follow your passion, and soon you start receiving thoughts creating doubt in you, thoughts of fear. You are still going to your job and the collective thought field of that place which is risk averse, preferring security within the comfort zone rather than adventure and growth starts to pull you back and convinces you to stay there and not follow your passion. This is again the collective energy of the thought matrix influencing you. And if your calling is strong which means the ENERGY of the thoughts of your calling is stronger than the thoughts coming from the collective mind then you will be able to overcome it and follow your dreams, if not you will surrender to the ENERGY of the collective field.

- **Subconscious mind:** Beneath your conscious mind there is a very wide region of subconscious mind. All habits originate from the subconscious plane. Subconscious plane is more powerful than the conscious plane of existence. Our reaction to any situation happens through the conditioning of our conscious and subconscious mind. Depending on the conditioning of our conscious and subconscious mind we attract the types of thoughts from the collective mind that match our subconscious patterns and frequencies. So for example if you are more focussed on frequency of anger then automatically it will make grooves in your mind such that thoughts of matching frequency, which is anger, will pass through it more than thoughts of peace. Reticular Activation System is a great example of this.

Psychologists use this term a lot now and you might have experienced this as well. If you want to buy a new BMW then suddenly you start to see more BMWs everywhere around you. You might think that more and more people are buying BMWs now than say a week ago before you made this decision or developed a liking for BMWs. Actually its your reticular activation system at work. Its like Google it contains information about trillions of websites and web pages, however the particular keyword you type it filters only the pages matching the keyword and your view of the internet gets restricted to the pages matching that.

- **Conscious mind:** Yes of course your conscious mind too is a source of your thoughts. Infact it is the only source over which you have direct control you can control and direct your mind to think thoughts of a particular type, on a particular subject or about a person. This is where both analytical and creative thinking comes into place. You can use your left brain and think logically or use the right brain and trigger thoughts of creativity. And you use this part of your brain to influence and control over the other sources of thoughts. This is where your true power resides. You can reprogram your subconscious mind by consistently thinking in the direction you want to go. By constantly feeding your subconscious with new information through reading, listening and contemplating you entertain thoughts of a particular desire you want to achieve and once it gets programmed you start to master that subject. So you are consciously choosing thoughts of a particular type to match the situation you are in. It is through the conscious mind you can make choices such that the collective thought field is also conducive to what you want to achieve.

By choosing to hang out with people who are also entertaining similar type of thoughts and hanging out at places where the collective field is also of a similar type you can consciously cultivate the thoughts you want to entertain in your mind.

Power Of Company

They say that your income is the average of the 5 people you hang out the most with. Why is it so, it's the energy of the collective thought field that is influencing you. Every time you come close to a person their energy field influences your energy field. Without you being aware of it. Yes and you might be thinking that this thought of doubt is your own original thought but it actually has just popped in from your friend who is full of fear. And in such interactions the person whose energy is the most dominant wins and influences all the people whose energy is weaker than him. So if you are much more positive than your friend then it would be the other way wherein you might inspire him. This has been scientifically studied also. A group of westerners were sent to spend time with some Buddhist monks, and every day there brain waves were studied. Just by being in the company of the peaceful monks (without doing any meditations themselves), the brain waves of the subjects saw considerable movement in the Alpha and Beta stages which are the brain wave frequency of deep relaxation and peace. So choose your company wisely because you don't know whose thought frequencies you are absorbing ☺.

How to control your thoughts

Thoughts cannot be controlled directly. They are too subtle to exercise direct power on them. There is a very interesting story that explains this. There was a princess that was caught and locked at the top of a tower with no access to it. The prince came to rescue her but was not sure how to get up there, how to climb the tower. He saw ants climbing up the tower. He had a rope but that were too heavy for the ants to carry up. Then an idea struck him, he tied a small thread to one of the ants. As the ant went up the light small thread also went up with it. The princess picked the thread up through the window of the top chamber of tower. Then the prince standing on the ground picked another thread that was slightly heavier than the earlier one but not too heavy. He tied this heavier thread to the thread the other end of which the princess was now holding. And the princess slowly pulled up the bigger, heavier and stronger thread. Now again the Prince repeated the same thing, hanging a slightly stronger thread each time and asking the Princess to pull up the more stronger thread with the help of the lesser one. Soon he was able to send the strong rope up to the Princess using, which she could come down and be rescued. So the moral of the story is that just like the Prince could not send the rope straight away to the Princess he had to use the lighter threads first similarly we can control the big jolts of thoughts directly by our physical will. However we can control our breath through our physical will. This breath is like that small starting thread that will eventually enable the heavy rope of mind to be pulled. But you have to start gradually with your breath. Through your breath you can conquer your mind. That is why Yoga lays so much emphasis on breathing and the importance of deep regulated breathing. Besides the energetic aspect of the breathing that we shared in earlier chapter this is the other aspect of breath in terms of its linkage to the mind, to the thoughts coming in the mind. If you observe your selves or others closely you can see matching patterns between your breath and thinking. The shallower the breath the more dispersed the mind, full of thoughts running around like loose canons in a battlefield. The deeper the breath you take the smaller the number of thoughts. And this is visible even other wise when you experience certain emotional states such as anger, the thoughts triggered generate a response of fast and shallow breathing. At that moment when you are angry if you focus on your breath and make it slow and deep you can immediately feel that your thoughts and emotions of anger will subside.

Exercise: Trataka

Drishti, a Sanskrit word, which means seeing is instrumental in controlling the movement of your thoughts in your mind. It is being scientifically proven that if you still your eyes or fix your eyes then it has a direct effect on your mind and it quietens it. Eyes are one of the most important sense organ that influences the mind. That is why almost all meditations and relaxation exercises require you to close your eyes (and not your ears or mouth or nose ☺). There is an ancient yogic practice that utilises this principle and helps with control of mind and thoughts. Its called Tratak. It requires gazing at an object or at a point steadily without blinking. This practice steadies the mind and enhances concentration. It can be done as follows:

- Sit comfortably on a chair or cross-legged on the floor.

- Lighten a candle in front of you such that the flame is at your eye level.

- Keep your spine straight and inhale and exhale deeply 5 times to bring the mind at rest.

- Now start gazing at the flame of the candle, concentrate on the middle of the flame and just focus on seeing. Do not try to analyse the flame or the candle or what you are doing just SEE.

- As you focus on the flame your mind will slowly start to quieten, you might have a few thoughts passing by your mind. That is fine. Let them pass by. Do not energise them either by controlling or entertaining them. Stay focused with your gaze on the flame of the candle.

- One minute of gazing is good to start with. Do not strain the eyes, if they feel sore close them immediately and start gazing again.

- This has a powerful affect on your mind bringing it to stillness.

Chapter 5:
Emotions as Energy

Do you want to FEEL absolutely amazing all the time and stay joyfully connected to your inner feelings?

Do you want to shift your health and happiness to a new level by expanding your understanding of emotions?

We are taught since childhood to repress our feelings and suppress our emotions. Certain emotions are labelled as good and some as bad. Moreover there is a gender bias with respect to emotions. If you are a female you are encouraged to be patient and not express anger or stand for your-self and be assertive. If you are a male then you have to be strong all the time. Men are expected not cry and should not display any soft emotions such as grief or hurt or even compassion. When you have suppressed and closed off your feelings you loose contact with your inner self. This limits your experience and joy of being alive.

The right way to deal with the energy of emotions

Emotions are actually energy in motion. You can empower yourself and increase your energy by feeling and experiencing positive emotions such as love, joy, happiness, enthusiasm, playfulness, and excitement or you can lower down your energy by leaking it through the experience of negatively vibrating emotions such as fear, hatred, guilt, sadness, and despair. How many times have you felt energetic and yet sad, none, right? How many times have you felt exuberant happy, excited but low in energy? Never, true. Frequency of emotion is in direct proportion to the energy you experience in your life.

The absolute right way to deal with your emotions is very very simple and yet we are taught all the time how to complicate it. We are taught all the time how to hide our emotions, not to express them. Men are conditioned since childhood not to cry or express compassion and warmth as these are considered to be symptoms of weakness. Women are taught not to be assertive, not to express their opinion or anger. All this clogs up emotions as well as energy. The right way to deal with emotions is to FEEL them. Yes feel them.

Its simple. It is that's for what they have been created. In fact in ancient yogic philosophy the life is considered synonymous to an ocean of emotions, *bhavsagar* as called in Sanskrit. And truly it is, what else have you done since you were born except experience certain set of emotions. As a kid you experience love of your parents, as adults love for your wife/partner and your children or the happiness over your achievements and sadness over your failures. You are just chasing emotions behind each and every achievement. You are not buying the BMW car because it's just a CAR that can take you from A to B. You are buying it for the emotion it will bring, how it will make you feel. Isn't that true? And yet you program yourself to hide your emotions, not express them fully or even worse express them incorrectly or inappropriately in order to manipulate others for small gains.

Energy of Love

Love is the primary emotion and in fact the only emotion in its true sense. All other emotions are gradation of this single emotion. In spirituality the entire universe is created out of single energy and that is the energy of Love. This is the only emotion that exists in reality. Just like the fact that light exists, darkness does not. It is absence of light that we experience as darkness.

Similarly fear, anger, hatred, jealousy, sadness and resentment are all emotions that arise from lack of the primary energy of love to various degrees. At a lower frequency love is experienced as happiness, at a still lower frequency as joy, still lower as sadness. Resentment, anger, guilt, shame and fear all are outcomes of absence of love in larger and larger quantities. The pure energy of love vibrating in lower frequency gives rise to other emotions that we experience which means that each emotion has a frequency of its own.

The better you feel the better life becomes, the worse you feel the worse your life becomes. Until you change the underlying emotions of how you feel you cannot change your life. It's the energy of the emotions you are feeling that drive your life towards success or failure. Feelings are the lowest common denominator to your life. When you feel good your thoughts are good, when your thoughts are good your words and actions i.e. the physical components are equally good and aligned.

Story of Nachiketa

In one of the ancient Vedic scripture Kathopanishada there is an interesting story of a young boy called Nachiketa. Interestingly his ignorant father under the influence of greed and anger offered him, his own son, to Yama, the god of death. Nachiketa being innocent but very wise asked Yama, the god of death the question, why does one has no suffering in Heaven, why does no one has any disease in Heaven.

Yama was quite perplexed with the questions of the young boy and explained him that in Heaven everyone vibrates with the feelings of unconditional love and gratitude that is why there is no disease and no suffering. The story clearly signifies that if you want to lead a healthy, disease free and happy life you need to cultivate and operate from the feelings of unconditional love and gratitude. Every time you bring in a feeling of a lower vibration we lower our energy towards disease. And moreover you need to purify your energetic system of these lower vibrations and not run away or hide from them, as that is worse.

Emotional Blockages

Every time you are untrue to an emotion, by repressing it or not feeling it appropriately you are creating an energy blockage that gets stored in your energy body forever. This restricts the flow of energy and only energy that resonates within the blockage is allowed to enter. This means that if you keep repressing anger or expressing it inappropriately then an energetic blockage gets created in your body, which invites more incidents for you to react with anger, and you become an anger experiencing machine. You start experiencing more and more anger on trivial incidents, thereby burning your energy through the low frequency emotion of anger. Moreover the energy of these unfelt emotions remain blocked in your body. This initially causes emotional and physical discomfort and if not released eventually leads to physical illness and disease. Psychotherapists agree that the cause of a most and probably all of the physical diseases is psychosomatic. Feelings of anger affect your liver; guilt and suppression lead to thyroid issues; and, hurt and sadness affects the functioning of your heart, and so on.

How to connect to your feelings

Throughout your day or ideally in the morning, bring your awareness to your heart centre in the middle of your chest and ask yourself 'How am I feeling right now?' Try to differentiate between your thoughts and feelings. Feelings would be generally a sum total of all the thoughts you are experiencing. So ask yourself and focus on the feelings rather than thought. Are you feeling peaceful, sad, happy, exuberant, anxious, angry, frustrated, guilty, loving? If the feeling is not clear try to give it a voice. Ask the feeling to talk to you and bring it to the surface. Become loving and supportive towards your feelings.

Try to expand your vocabulary and experience of feeling. It goes hand in hand your expression and feeling. If you cannot express in words what your are feeling, you cannot feel that feeling clearly and completely. Most of your experiences are limited to the expression you can give them in the form of words. So expand your vocabulary of experiences and that will expand your horizon of living.

Emotions and Chakras

So are there any specific places where these emotional blockages reside in the energy body? The answer is yes; predominantly, the emotional blockages are stuck in your Chakras, which are the vortex of cosmic energy flowing into our system. The seven chakras inside the human body are linked with our emotional body and simulate specific types of emotions and their malfunctioning can also cause serious emotional blockages. Once your chakras go out of balance, the energy gets blocked; the life force in you slows down. You may feel tired, depressed and restless. The mind and thought processes get affected and diseases also get manifested. Doubt, fear and negative attitude may preoccupy you.

Mooladhar or Survival Centre

When this chakra is blocked, certain emotions are felt such as frustration, insecurity, and anxiety. Emotional issues that block the energy include feeling of danger and insecurity, and feeling of mistrust. There is also a feeling of being alienated from the rest of the world. You perceive yourself as not belonging to anyone or anywhere and may find it difficult to be grounded and practical. You lack the energy to get things done in a timely manner and even small challenges seem too big to overcome.

Swadhisthan the Passion Centre

If this Chakra is out of balance, there will be emotional problems related to passion, joy, and creativity. There will be addiction to feelings of guilt, self-denial, and the inability to receive without a feeling of being obliged. You will not feel good about who you are. There will be uncertainty, indecisiveness, constantly questioning regarding what to do. There is also struggle in giving and taking and becoming passive and assertive.

Manipura the Power Centre

This centre revolves primarily around issues relating to fear. When this chakra is not balanced, certain emotions are observed such as worry, confusion, depression, and lack of confidence. There can also be a lack of self-esteem, fear of rejection, defensiveness even around constructive criticism, and, being secretive and indecisive. The emotional blockages or issues that block the energy causes challenges with respect to self-respect, making decisions, defensiveness, and competitiveness.

Anahat the Heart Centre

Having a blocked Heart Chakra implies ego problems and lack of love for self and for others. If this is blocked you will not trust anyone and always have a shield around you. It is a projection of inner lack of self-love, acceptance, and trust like closing the door on everything that is warm and beautiful. Primarily the emotions of hurt, sadness, and grief block this chakra and take you away from the prime life force energy of unconditional love.

Vishuddhi the Self Expression Centre

If this Chakra is blocked, how you appear to others would be quite different to who you really are. This could possibly cause lot of misunderstandings in life. It is much better to express what you really feel than to pretend yourself as someone you are not. It causes issues that relate to our personal expression, how others see you, your personality and how our creative self-expression shines out into the world. Every time you express yourself incorrectly or inappropriately you create an energetic blockage in this chakra.

Ajna the Decision Centre

If you have a blocked 6th Chakra, you will find it hard to trust your inner voice. You will find it difficult to make decisions, procrastinate a lot, and would not be clear what you really want. It can make you quite superstitious and afraid of your own thoughts and emotions. You will find it hard to be practical and grounded in day-to-day life. There will be no balance and you might develop victim mentality, become irresponsible and blame everything on someone or something else.

Sahasrar the Spiritual Centre

A malfunctioning Crown Chakra can cause self-centeredness, poor perception and control on reality, and low energy level all the time. There will be difficulty in concentrating and thinking clearly about things. People with a blocked and underactive Sahasrar have scattered mentality and lack of future goals. They are definitely not visionaries and just busy thinking about what they need to do the next day. They struggle for having a clearer sense of purpose. Such person will be in a constant state of chaos and confusion regarding himself and others. A feeling of emptiness exists with no boundaries, no rules, and such people are generally nervous and confused on everything.

Meditation to release blocked emotions

- Close your eyes, relax and sit straight with your spine straight. Connect with your breath, and start taking deep slow breath. Inhale from your nose and exhale from your mouth.

- Now become aware of your heart, this is the place where we experience most of our emotions. Imagine with your eyes closed that the heart expands into a closed room and you can enter that.

- Imagine you are in the room safe and secure with no one else to watch you, no one else to care about except just yourself. Within the safety of this room ask yourself what is the most important emotion that you need to heal? Don't think just ask and the first emotion that comes to your mind, pick that up.

- It could be Anger; it could be Fear or Sadness. Whatever it is, welcome it. Rather than running away from it bring it to your awareness.

- Now start feeling this emotion. Bring it out in you deliberately, feel it intensely. If it reminds you of a time when you felt this emotion the most but could not express it, bring that situation out in your mind and relive it. If its anger, relive that anger, allow your body to shake, your eyes to become full of tears if need be but bring it out and feel it completely. You are safe and secure in the chamber of your heart so don't hesitate; let the emotion run completely through you.

- If your consciousness brings in some people let it do so, feel the repressed emotion against these persons within the chamber of your heart where it is safe to do so. If your breathing intensifies let it do so, breathe deeply to increase your energy for the release of this emotion. You are not this emotion you are the experiencer of this emotion, the witness of this experience, realise that, and detach yourself with the emotion but yet feel it.

- Now slowly start coming back move your fingers, slowly open your eyes. You will feel like a big burden is off your shoulder.

- Relax and thank yourself and if your emotion involved in any way with you not living up to your expectation then forgive yourself, consider it as a learning experience for you to evolve as a better human being and start loving your self even more.

Chapter 5 : Emotions as Energy

- If you saw another person in your release thank them as well and also forgive them now completely, Consider them as an instrument of the universe to teach you a lesson that was important for your growth. Forgive them and release any grudge that you were holding against them. The release you have done would automatically reduce the emotional charge from your mind so you will find it much easier to do that now. Forgive them and accept them the way they are so that you can move on in your journey of life, of personal evolution and growth.

Chapter 6:
Words as Energy

Do you want to feel confident, positive, and hopeful when you speak?

Do you want to be able to create wonderful relationships all around you?

Every word you speak is a mathematical program that manipulates and programs the reality with its energy. Whatever you say matters, so be very careful of what you say. Just like thoughts, words create reality. In fact it never happens in isolation, words are energised by the emotions and thoughts behind them. The higher and stronger the emotion behind a particular word you speak, the stronger will be the energy it contains to influence the reality. If you are constantly complaining, whining and cribbing, you are creating a reality that resonates with that. The energy of those thoughts, feelings, and words will act as a mathematical program that makes the people listening to it as well as those not listening to it a reality act in such a way that they bring back to you the same frequency of reality that you spoke. The energy of the words you speak, first affects your mind, by creating neuro-pathways that matches it. Then it influences the listener to act in a certain way that matches that frequency. And simultaneously it creates ripples across the subtle thought matrix that I spoke about in the last chapter in such a way that people, places, and situations that match the frequency start gravitating towards you. That's why they say energy attracts like energy. So you continue to stay in the similar situation still complaining, whining, and cribbing.

The other aspect of your reality being influenced by words is through what you listen to. The words you listen to constantly program your mind. They create the neuro-pathways, which then influence your behaviours, your choices, and ultimately what you speak. If you constantly bombard yourself with negative words, words of failure, chaos, resentment, desperation then the energy of these words will impact your mind significantly. That is why it is advised not to listen to news channels or read newspapers much. The news these days package a whole bunch of negativity from the remotest corners of the world to the comfort of your home where you can easily consume all negativity and lock it inside your energy anatomy for decades ☺. I am not kidding, isn't that what's happening? In my personal experience of the recession of 2007, the news instruments almost announced the end of the world in multiple ways. Everyday there was news of what bad is happening or what worse could happen. And you take all that into your psycho energetic system in the form of awareness. You need to be more aware of where your own energy is going. Is it increasing and taking you towards your higher self, your higher purpose, and your higher goals or is it diminishing with more and more energy blockages being programmed into your energetic anatomy.

A word of caution here is about what you speak to your children. Never speak to them in a negative way even if you are trying to motivate them. You are programming their reality through the words you speak to them. The energetic impact of the words stays in their consciousness and in the thought matrix as well long after those words have been spoken.

You could be living a reality that was influenced by the words spoken to you as a child. Your parents, your teachers and other family members have all contributed to the energetic patterns that exist within you in the form of your thought and feeling. A child brought up with love, appreciation, and tenderness exhibits those traits throughout his life. Scientific studies show that till the age of nine, children have their minds in Alpha state, which is the highly suggestible state where the brain waves are quite slow enhancing learning. So please take this word of advice to enhance the reality of those around you, specially your children.

Dr Emoto's Words are alive water experiment

Masaru Emoto is a Japanese author and researcher known for his famous experiments on effect of words and emotions on the molecular structure of water. His research shows that the human vibrational energy expressed in the form of words, thoughts and emotions affects the structure of water. In his experiment he placed water in different bottles and on each bottle he put a label with a word written on in such as Love, Hate, and so on. The bottles were then frozen so that the water inside would form crystalline structure. He even taped names such as Hitler and Mother Teresa, or phrases such as 'You make me sick' or 'Thank You for your kindness' on various bottles. In bottles having the positive meaning words and phrases the crystalline structure of water was well organised, beautiful, and coherent. Whereas for the water that was labelled with negative words and phrases the crystalline structure was haphazard, discordant, and unorganised. This clearly demonstrated through scientific experiments that words have the power to influence reality. Imagine if the words and thoughts that come out of us have such an effect on water crystals, what kind of effect they can have on the people and events in our lives.

Affirmations

An affirmation is a positive thought or word that you repeat to yourself. Using affirmations allows you to select the quality of your thoughts and implant them into your subconscious. You can use affirmations to get results in a variety of areas:
For example while playing golf you can say:
"I will play a good game."

Chapter 6 : Words as Energy

For improving your relationships you can say:
"Everyone treat me with love and respect, and I treat myself and everyone with equal love and respect."

It is most effective to practice affirmations before going to sleep and just after waking up. Those are the times when your brain is in Alpha state i.e. the brain waves are considerably slow, which lower the conscious mind so whatever you affirm goes directly into your subconscious mind and programs it. This makes a lasting impact of the affirmation on your personality as the chatter of the conscious mind, which acts as an inhibitor to access the subconscious mind is down. This is a similar state that hypnotists take you to when they try to release sub conscious pattern or create a new pattern to help you in quitting, say smoking. They are using the energy of words to change the energetic programs in your mind that are influencing your choices and actions. If they don't say anything when you are in Alpha state you don't change, that is why words are the energy that shifts your neuro-pathways, your thinking patterns.

There are certain rules that make affirmations work better: -

- Unless you back the affirmations with feelings they are powerless. Feelings provide the required energy and fuel for affirmation to work. The stronger the feeling behind the words the higher the energy, hence the faster and bigger the shift the affirmation can produce.

- Two negatives do not produce a positive with affirmations. You subconscious and collective mind do not understand grammar of negation. If you say I will not argue or I will not be sad, then it ignores the negation in the sentence and the result is you will ARGUE, you will feel SAD. Instead you need to make the affirmation simple and positive such as: I will accept and appreciate different point of view, or I am Happy.

- Affirmations are more affective when you say them out loud or write them. The more senses you involve with the affirmations the easier it is to form new neuro-pathways.

- Repetition is important: If you want to restructure a deep rooted belief that you have had for 15 years then merely saying the affirmation 10 times a day for 15 days will not help. You need to counter the energetic blockage with equal amount of energy through POSITIVE, full or FEELINGS, SENSE Engaging and REPETITIVE affirmations.

Loss of energy

Just like haphazard thinking, haphazard talking, which predominantly includes gossip, causes a lot of loss to your vital life force energy. You might not be aware of it. It is not just physical fatigue and loss of energy I am talking about here but the loss of your core life force energy in the name of gossip or time pass. Plus if you are discussing about people and situations negatively or even mocking things just for your fun then you are sending strong vibrations into the thought matrix. Although you might be thinking that the person cannot hear you but still the energy of your conversation will reach him/her. This also creates a karmic balance between you and the other person. As per the law of karma the nature has to settle the energy exchange that you have started in one way or the other. The energy of your thoughts, emotions and words sent to other person has to come back to you in some form. And if your contribution in the thought matrix was negative you are bound to get back a negative energy consequence. And as we see later even money and disease are nothing but energy you are bound to settle for that debt in some form of energy exchange. So you see idle gossip has two disadvantages, namely, it contributes to significant loss of physical and mental energy and it causes karmic imbalances which you then have to pay back energetically in the form or money or disease or relationships.

Energy of Vishuddhi (Throat) Chakra: Uninhibited Self Expression

Talking about life force energy of words we speak, let us see how our Chakras influence our control on what we speak, how we speak, what comes out of our mouth and what is the energy implication for us. The health of this chakra influences how a person expresses himself/herself. According to researches, lying violates the spirit and body and since you express your choices with the use of your voice hence the throat chakra matters. All the choices that you usually make in your life have consequences on energy level. If you choose to speak out diplomatically while repressing your anger it can manifest itself into laryngitis. Most people already experience lump in their throats especially when they are at crossroads, not knowing the right words to speak on a specific occasion. Haven't you experienced this weird feeling in your throat when you are confused? The challenge of the throat chakra is to know the right way to express your-self in a truthful manner and at the same time be able to assimilate and receive information. It is very important to stay aligned with your truth.

The emotional blockages or issues that block the energy create conflicts between listening and speaking. If this Chakra is blocked, how you appear to others would be quite different than what you really are. This could possibly cause misunderstandings in life. It is much better to express what you really feel than to pretend yourself as someone you are not. It causes issues that relate to our personal expression, how others see you, our personality and how your creative self-expression shines out into the world.

Never complete a negative sentence about yourself or others

As mentioned earlier every word you speak is a mantra, or in modern language a mathematical program. It sets into motion your intention behind the spoken word and starts organizing the creative principle of the universe to deliver that to you. So be very careful of what you speak. Speak positive even if you are feeling negative or low. Never complete a single negative sentence about yourself. Rephrase it to sound positive. For example:

- Rather than saying' I can't do this', you can say' I choose not to do this'.
- Instead of saying 'It's difficult to achieve', say 'With required energy commitment and focus I can achieve my desires'.
- Instead of saying 'I can't afford this' say 'I am on my way and soon will be able to buy this'.

Use your words that empower yourself and others, words of encouragement and stay away from the words that take away your power or make others feel down, low and less. And often a very subtle difference in your choice of words can create a huge impact on you and the person you are communicating to. Words such as:

- You need to do this,
- You should do this, or
- You have to do this

Simply force rather than choice. People would have subconscious resistance to such words as they are disempowering. They take away the freedom of choice from the doer implying that you are doing it by force and so you don't feel responsible internally towards actions triggered by such words. No one HAS to do anything you are always choosing. Even though it might appear that you have to do something, for example you might say you have to work in order to feed your children. But if you look slightly deeper into it it's a choice that you are making, you can choose not to do it also, and it's just that the love and responsibility for your children is making you choose to work. One great example of power of words came from Nelson Mandela. When he was interviewed after coming out of the prison after 20 years, he was asked 'Nelson how did you survive in there?' and Nelson Mandela said 'young man you offend me. I did not survive, I chose to learn about my fellow human beings while I was in that place'. So if you want to empower yourself remove the words, I need to, I have to and replace them with I choose to, I am responsible for.

Cultivating awareness of speech

Words are wonderful when used in a proper way. They can encourage, edify and give confidence to the hearer. A right word spoken at right time can be life changing. You can increase your joy by speaking the right words. Some points to consider before speaking:

- Do you really have to give your opinion
- Say something good or don't say anything at all
- Use gentle words
- Keep your word
- Ask your higher self to help you speak the right thing.

Pay attention to how you feel when certain words are used. Do you feel confident, positive, and hopeful when you speak? Try switching out the negative words from your vocabulary. Get creative and find ways to only use positive, impactful words. Even in a negative situation, positive words can be used. For example, if you're sick and down with cold, having headache and if someone asks you how you're feeling, try saying something like, "I am looking forward to feeling like my old self again." Using words for the positive is so powerful! You'll be surprised how you feel and I guarantee those around you will appreciate the shift. Another example of using words of power is if, say your girlfriend is late and rather than blaming or shaming her with your words you can say something positive oriented such as I appreciate you when you are on time. Positive words uplift and establish a powerful sense of well-being. Doesn't everyone want to feel this?

Use optimistic, high energy words such as: Awesome, Beautiful, Happy, Positive, Easy, Free, Funny, Choose, Energy, Enthusiasm, Harmony, Success, Pure, Love, Thankful, Grateful, and so on.

Avoid using energy sucking words such as: I can't, I shouldn't, It's difficult, Failure, Guilt, Hate, Control, Fear, Problem, Sad, Sick, Weak, Worry, Lose, Broke, Complaint, Expensive, and so on.

Energy of sound – Mantras

Yoga is known to use mantras for specific purposes. In fact in Yoga they say Mantra Maheshwara or Mantra i.e. the energy of sound is equivalent to the energy of God or Creator. We mentioned about Chakras in the earlier part of this book. Chakras are vortices of energy and as you know they get blocked constricting the flow of energy passing through them. Chakras are activated using the energy of sound.

Each specific chakra has a corresponding sound that resonates with its frequency, a Mantra. When we chant that mantra the Chakra starts to vibrate and activate. Mantra meditation is a very profound way to concentrate your mind and increase your energy. As regards Breath Mantra So Ham, If you try to listen to your voice then it makes the sound of So Ham, So with inhalation and Ham with exhalation. If you focus on this sound with your breath it will energise you considerably as you are bringing in the energy of the mantra and the energy of the breath into your system. There are other specific mantras that create ripples in the universe and attract specific type of energy in your life for example:

- **Aim**: This is the mantra that resonates with the energy of learning, art and creativity. If you chant this mantra you will open your energy field to receive more knowledge and wisdom.

- **Shreem**: This is the mantra that resonates with the energy of abundance, wealth, money and prosperity. Chanting this mantra opens you to receive the energy of the universe in the form of money, wealth, and prosperity.

- **Dum:** This is the mantra that invokes the energy of protection. The complete mantra is **Om Dum Durgaye Namah.**

- **Namah Shivaya**: The energy of this five-syllable mantra uplifts your mood and purifies your mind of all the impurities and negativity. This mantra is very powerful and works with the lower five chakras purifying them and seriously impacting your life, your reality by purifying your desires, thoughts and action.

- **Gum Ganpataye Namah:** This is the mantra that brings good luck by removing the obstacles that might come in your path to achieve your desired results.

Exercise: Mauna

Yoga recommends a very powerful practice to conserve your energy and cultivate control over your speech. Practice staying silent for at least 30 minutes every day and then for a minimum of two hours every weekend and if possible for a full day every month. This first of all prevents loss of energy spent in talking and also helps cultivate awareness of speech, which eventually leads to control on speech. Another good exercise to practice for conserving sound energy is through silent walks. Go for a walk in the woods, or along a beach and for the entire duration of the walk practice Mauna or silence.

Chapter 7:
Money as Energy

Do you want to experience more wealth, more abundance and more prosperity?

Do you want to allow energy in the form of money to flow into your life?

If I ask you what is Money, what is the first thing that comes to your mind, Dollar bills, coins, gold, stocks and shares, bank accounts... and the list could go on and on. Is that true? Well the answer is NO. These are all expressions or outcomes of money. Money is not what is sitting in your bank account or in your investments. It is ENERGY in its true form. It is a symbol of your creative energy. We have created a system for the expression of this creative energy that everyone has in the form of pieces of paper or coins. You acquire the symbolic money in exchange of the energy you spent creating a product or delivering a service and then you trade that to exchange it with the energetic creation of other person or a group. The cars/bank balances/notes/coins are the expression of the exchange of this creative energy generated by different individuals. A shortage of money often stems from the fact that our creative energy is blocked in some way.

Myths about money

Money is the root of all evil. We have heard this statement so many times and so many times that this statement has got ingrained in our subconscious and programmed into us. Another stereotype is regarding Rich versus Poor - rich person is always bad and immoral while the poor guy has all the morals and ethics but no money. So is money really evil? Is it the root of all evil? The answer is simply NO. I mean now that you understand that money is nothing but energy. Can energy be evil? You can use it in an evil way just like nuclear energy can be used to light up a thousand households or to bomb an entire city; same way the energy of money can be used either positively or negatively. But **Money energy is essentially always NEUTRAL**. In fact the yogis have worshiped this universal energy of money in the form of Goddess

Chapter 7 : Money as Energy

Laxmi, who is depicted as pure, divine and unconditional.

Money is a neutral instrument for measuring exchange of energy based on common value agreed with it. It has the values that we give to it through our attitude and use of it. The energy of the universe takes on many forms of physical reality such as love, time, space, air, water, and food to name a few. And the funny thing is that you never say:

"It is bad to have more love in my life... or more time, or more air, water, food sunshine in my life".

You never ask for less love, less time, less food, air and water but with money you feel humble and good if you ask less of it. From an energetic perspective isn't this crazy but true?

The social conditioning around money is so powerful that for most people this energy form of universe is associated with fear. People fear money, they think that if they have more money they will become corrupt, unpleasant, bad, ruthless, and cunning. This again is not true. Putting it simply, **Money makes you more of what you already are.** So if you are already an alcoholic, money will make you more of an alcoholic, if you are already a gambler, money will make you a bigger gambler. On the other hand if you are already a saintly person like Mother Teresa, imagine what millions of dollars she raised did for her and humanity. In her case, money just amplified who she already was.

Money is the energetic means and not the end

The next shift required in understanding the energy of money is that it is a means and not an end. Yet the majority of humanity is chasing money just for the sake of it. I mean imagine would you store the light of sun or electricity or heat just for the sake of it, NO. Every time you feel lack of money or a desire for more money, ask your- self for what purpose you need it. Your WHY for money is considerably important. There is nothing wrong with having more money, as much as you want, as long as you know its purpose. Imagine spending your valuable years chasing money without knowing your specific purpose for it and then at the end of your life realizing that you missed on so many other joys and experiences that life has to offer. The experiences that you wanted to experience, the change that you want to create in your life and in the lives of others is what you need Money for. If your why is not clear then you might be pursuing money energy for the wrong ends that are not fulfilling to you.

Think of what specific energy exchange you want to achieve with your money energy. Become clear of your goals and then determine how much of money energy you need to accomplish them and then go for it with your heart, mind, and soul.

Align Money with Love

It is important to connect with others to exchange your creative energy with them and in return get their creative energy in the form of money. So the more you connect with others and the more you add value to their lives through your energy, your gifts, your skills, and talents, the more Money energy you attract in your life. You get what you want from life by helping others get what they want from life. It is just that simple. All this springs from their core desire to serve others to the best of their ability. The core difference to manifest more money energy is in motivation. If your motivation is more than just money you will succeed more. If you link your motivation to service and love, it will be much easier and fulfilling to achieve your money goals. And this is a very logical proposition. As I told you, all energy in this universe including the energy of money is another form of unconditional love energy. Love is the most powerful force in the universe and if you align your motivation and business to the energy of love, then that goal will be fulfilled abundantly and the money will flow like water!

Your Chakras are blocking your Money Energy

This is very interesting and you might be thinking what does money have to do with Chakras. Chakras are the major life force energy centers and money is also another form of energy so there is definitely a connection. And you will be surprised to know that a blockage in a particular chakra might be the cause for your not being able to manifest as much money in your life as you would like to. Your attitude about money and what it signifies to you determines which chakra will influence the flow of money energy in your life.

If you are primarily looking at money to feel safe and secure then it will be your Mooladhar chakra that is influencing how much money you have. If there are blockages in your Mooladhar chakra then you will find it difficult to manifest more money and will only be able to use money to seek safety and security in your life rather than other pursuits such as passion or love, which are represented by the higher chakras. If on the other hand you look at money as a means for sensual enjoyment, passion and creativity then it is the Swadhisthan Chakra that is influencing its flow in your life. A healthy and open Swadhisthan chakra will mean you will create more of the energy of money in your life. You will create more money by pursuing your passion and use it to find joy in life.

And finally the third chakra, Manipura influences your money energy if you associate money with power. If you like to show off with your money, buy things that increase your status symbol, then it is the Manipura chakra that is associated with Money. If it is open you will have good leadership qualities, higher self-esteem and self-confidence and will use these to manifest more money in your life.

Your Karmic patterns are blocking your Money Energy

With every thought we create, word we speak and action we do, Karma is created. This Karma gets stored in our subtle body and guides our psyche and behavior. It influences our thinking pattern and eventually the choices that we make. As we are the sum total of all the choices we have made in the past, we are a sum total of the Karma we have created. Moreover we all have karmic patterns that we inherit from our parents. Under the influence of these we continuously make same choices again and again. We find ourselves making the same choices that our parents made and almost feel guilty in making different choices. So if your parents had a particular programming about money that money is evil or if your father had spent his life with certain beliefs about money, how to make money, how much to charge for it you will inherit the same energy programs in your system. This is the reason most of the people do not break the earning barriers that are set by their parents.

Examples of Karmic patterns:

- I don't deserve so much.
- I am not worth it.
- I can't do it. I am not good enough.
- I lack the resources and have limitations.
- If I earn more money than my parents then I am not a good son or daughter.
- I am a victim everyone takes advantage of me.

It is very important to get rid of these deep-rooted energy blockages in order to allow you to make choices that welcome the energy of money in your life.

Allow the energy to flow

Money is the kinetic energy of universe; it loves to flow rather than being static. If you want more of it then better become a channel such that it can flow through you. Rather than hoarding and blocking this energy share it with others. Allow it to flow through you and you will receive more and more of it. This shifts your mindset from lack and limitation to abundance. Charity is a great way to do this. When you share with others what you have without any expectation in return, it sends a powerful signal to the universe that you have more than enough and the universe in return gives you more. Isn't that a wonderful position to be in? Another important effect charity has on you is that it purifies the energy of your money. We live in a Karma operated world and it is very difficult to settle the karma of give and take perfectly. There will be times where you would have taken more than you gave in a particular energy exchange scenario. This creates a karmic debt which you will have to repay in some way in the future and that might cost you much more in the form of bad health, bad luck, and, unforeseen and unnecessary expenses. If we keep doing charity then that karmic debt created unknowingly by you will keep getting settled. This will allow universe to flood your life with more life force energy in the form of money.

Exercise: Bless your money

Whatever you bless and appreciate with pure intention increases manifold in energy, this is the law of life force energy. If you bless your food and feel grateful for it, the life force energy of it increases manifold, and, the nutrition and satisfaction we receive from it is unmatched.

Similarly when you bless your money energy and feel grateful that it is present in your life, this too increases the flow of this energy in your life manifold and you get richer and richer. The more you bless and feel grateful about it the more easily it appears in your life. However money is slightly different to food. It is kinetic life force energy where as food is static life force energy. With money you have to bless it whenever you receive it and spend it. You bless it by feeling grateful about it whenever you receive it. And everytime you spend it, whether for a cup of coffee, or lunch, grocery, shopping, petrol, and so on, silently bless it. Feel thankful for it and then think of all the lives that will be positively impacted by your purchase. Give all the people through whose hands this energy flows give a silent blessing along with the money. This is a very, very powerful exercise for shifting your money vibration, your attitude about money and its energy. Try this for a few days and notice the difference ☺

Money Affirmations

Change your self-talk when it comes to Money. Here are some affirmations that can help you change your relationship with money energy.

- I love and appreciate money as simply energy and greatly appreciate this energy for enhancing my life.
- I have a healthy and balanced relationship with money and strongly believe money is a positive and wonderful energy of the Universe.
- I am very grateful that I can use money as a tool to create my perfect lifestyle and experience my hearts desires.
- I trust that the universal life force energy provides me with all the opportunities to be abundant in my finances.
- I completely enjoy giving and receiving money and acknowledge its abundance.
- I am confident in my ability to create any amount of income I choose.
- I feel good and empowered when I generously share my money with others.
- I am happily grateful for the freedom, choices and abundance that money brings to me.
- I am deeply grateful for my financial freedom.
- I am receiving inspiration to create new ways of manifesting more abundance in my life.
- I eagerly ask the Universe to show me new and inspiring opportunities for manifesting more life force energy in the form of money.

Conclusion: Transforming Your Energy

Yaa Devi Sarva Bhuteshu Shakti Rupena Samsthita
Namestasyai Namestasyai Namestasyai Namoh Namah

O' Mother Universe who pervades everything in the form of Energy
I bow to you, I bow to You, I bow to You
~Devi Mahatmayam

Life Force Energy

We are all filled with the all-pervading cosmic life force energy. This energy is the essence of our life and our existence. We experience life as this energy flows through the various levels of our being such as the physical, the mental, the emotional and the spiritual. During the course it can become unbalanced, blocked and uneasy in flow. When this happens we experience what we call as dis-ease. Dis-ease as it suggests is the inability of the life force energy to freely flow in a particular aspect of life.

This unbalanced and blocked energy manifests in the form of physical health issues and karmic patterns that prevents us from making choices that can allow us to live with more abundance, harmony and happiness. In the physical body an energetic blockage will create disease such as headaches, diabetes, arthritis, or cancer. In the emotional body the dis-ease of energy will cause, depression, stress, anger, and phobias. In the mental body it will inhibit us from thinking positively and responding creatively to situations and circumstances. In the spiritual body it will manifest as materialism, being narrow minded and narrow sighted, disrespect for nature.

Evolution is the core principle of life, we are all born so that we can evolve further into a better human being than we already are until we reach the perfection that is infinite, until we become one with GOD who is the infinite. And in order to evolve these energetic blockages must be overcome, must be removed. Removing these blockages means changing how we perceive ourselves and the world around us. As we evolve we start realizing our higher selves, which is not just physical in dimension, and realize that the essence of our higher self is pure unconditional love.

Working with the energy body is the fastest way to heal these blockages at all levels. Some blockages might be bigger and take more time to heal than others. However one pre requisite to healing your energy is your willingness to release the stagnant unwanted energy. Only then you can experience its affects on physical, emotional, or spiritual levels. Unless you allow your self to release the unwanted energy it will stay there. Even GOD will not be able to heal you without your consent. Knowingly or unknowingly you yourself have created these blockages and unless you give permission to your self to heal and release these blockages they will not go.

Auric clearing and Chakra healing are one of the best ways to get rid of these unwanted energetic blockages from your system. If you look at the testimonials I have helped so many people heal at different levels, from emotional issues prohibiting them to bring love in their lives to mental blockages curing stress and depression to supporting recovery from physical diseases such as cancer.

All healing happens through the energy of Unconditional Love. We are all infact the entire universe is created out of the energy of unconditional love. Whenever we deviate or go against unconditional love we create an energetic blockage within us. These energetic blockages can only be dissolved through the energy of unconditional love. In my healing sessions I use the energy of unconditional love to transform and transmute the source of the blockages.

Yoga and meditation are the ways through which you can maintain good health of your energy body. A healthy energy body means a healthy physical body, a happy emotional body and a positive and sharp mind.

People always ask me how to meditate, and what type of meditation to practice. The most popular forms of meditation is mindfulness meditation. However I recommend chakra meditation to start with. And there is a simple reason for that. Mindfulness is an outcome that is achieved when your mind becomes calm and focused. Until your chakras are cleared of the blockages you will find it very hard to achieve mindfulness. Imagine a house with seven rooms and in each room there are four or five naughty kids playing and making noise. Can you meditate in that house, or stay peaceful and calm. No isn't it? That is why unless the 7 rooms of your energy body are cleared you will find it difficult to achieve mindfulness and meditation.

Tips on Meditation

Meditate daily ideally twice a day or at least once, either in the morning or evening. It is important to transfer our sensory control internally as external realities leave us very little or not connected with the inner being, which happens to be the source of all peace, happiness and guidance arise. Daily meditation helps to clear the mental chatter that we pick during our daily routine. Meditation is a supplement to sleep as during slumber we simply loose awareness. Hence meditation proves more beneficial than just regular sleeping for relaxation and proper control of mind.

Choose the same time and same place for meditation. Every day if you meditate on the same place and at the same time then it has a spiraling effect on your meditation and it becomes deeper and stronger. This is for two reasons; first, the place where you meditate regularly accumulates the peaceful vibrations generated during meditation so next time when you start you leverage your past vibrations. It is important that the place for meditation be chosen either as an independent room or some corner of the room where no one walks through frequently. Second, as a pavlovian reflex your mind becomes conditioned and receptive to the state of meditation and practicing at the same time everyday make it easier for you to enter the state of meditation and reach the climax.

Remember, meditation cannot be practiced mechanically as it is a state of being and not doing, it happens, you can only achieve that by creating a conducive outward and inward environment through regular practice with recommended steps and conditions. Ideally meditation **should be done on empty stomach** or after a considerable gap after eating and never immediately after meals. This is so because after eating most of the blood gets directed to your stomach to help in digestion so less blood flows through your brain and it becomes difficult for you to stay alert which is what makes meditation different from sleep, i.e. in meditation you are relaxed but alert which is not possible if stomach is full.

There is a difference between meditation and relaxation. Most people believe both are same. It is not true. Both are different though highly inter-related and capable of reinforcing each other. It implies that one should be relaxed in order to be able to meditate and regular meditation keeps your mind relaxed and healthy. So in meditation, you start with relaxation but as said earlier, during meditation you are also get aware of your inner self, Your presence except for the mental chatter becomes nil or negligible, depending on the type of meditation you are doing which may involve concentrating completely on some mantra or some task. So relaxation is a prerequisite for meditation and sleep, both of which are two different states of existence. Hence meditation should not be done while lying down as it will definitely lead to sleep. It has to be done in a sitting posture either on a chair or sitting cross legged, which is an energy generating posture and facilitates better meditation. Always keep your spine straight allowing easy flow of energy across your nervous system.

… Life Force Energy

I Can Help You!!

Testimonials

Puneet helped me by teaching me how to meditate and breathe properly, specific asanas to keep my root and heart chakras more balanced and quite a lot of healing. I always felt lighter in my mind after each session. He also gave me a lot of guidance and a really good schedule to keep my chakras balanced. I previously did a lot of Yoga and breathing exercises but that wasn't enough. Puneet was able to put it all together for me just like a puzzle so that I could properly heal. The result was that I now feel really grounded and I rarely feel any anxiety. I used to take calming herbal tablets to keep my anxiety at bay but no longer feel the need to take any. One thing I really liked was the auric clearing; it balances all of your chakras so I felt amazing as if a lot of weight had been lifted.
This experience was truly life changing. I would recommend Puneet to any one who needs some healing physically and emotionally and is looking for positive changes in their lives.

Catherine Biewer - Sales Manager, London

Puneet's chakra meditation has helped me achieve more balance and grounding. I feel more relaxed and cantered during my day now and full of energy. It has helped me manage my stress and also stay more focussed. Meditation has helped improve my overall productivity. I will recommend Puneet and his meditation techniques to everyone who wants to improve their energy levels and concentration and reduce their stress.

Kam Dovedi - CEO Premier Portfolio Builder, London

Puneet's meditation and breathing techniques helped me recover from stress and depression. I was in a phase of my life where my career was not going as I had planned and there was a lot of stress. I was not enjoying my work and had started feeling purposeless even though I had a good job that most people would envy and a healthy loving family. Puneet told me that the problem was with my energy being too low for me too appreciate the good things in life. His Chakra meditation helped me recover from the stress and brought back balance into my life. The energy healing of chakras and my auras had an immediate affect on my energy, my mood and my sleep. He taught me how to maintain that energy so that stress and depression never come back. The result is that now I am rocking in my career and am enjoying my time with family and friends much more than before. Any time a challenge comes I know that I have the energy to handle it completely and comfortably. I would recommend Puneet's healing and meditation to everyone who wants to achieve success in their career and in life.

Amit Sharma - Investment banker, India

I felt peaceful and lifted in my consciousness, my mind felt opened and clearer.

Abi: London Om Yoga Show

Lovely resonating vibrations of mantras through the core of the body.

Ianthe: London Om Yoga Show

I had a great experience and felt vibrations in my throat chakra, third eye and on my head. Certainly worth trying :-)

Caroline: London Om Yoga Show

I Can Help You!!

Thank you very much for the clearing. Here is my experience: I felt very tired after our session of aura/chakra clearing. Which I took as a good sign and was prepared for ... straight to bed. The day or two the surrounding energy was a bit heavy, but with a subtle "ok" feeling intuitively.

I have an amazing dream the second night. I dropped seeds on the ground, not necessary fertile ground, hard ground, which was clearly noted. They instantly started sprouting and growing fast in front of my eyes. Vine like limbs twisting and twining then.... beautiful flowers, lot of different brilliant colours (looking a bit like a Wisteria), making different shapes. Dropping more seeds and watching how it quickly it sprouted and grew.... The flowers never stopped coming.. dropping and growing non-stop. My garden was full of spring flowers & colours .. all around me. My whole being filled with joy and happiness ... I shouted out in happiness. In my garden was only spring (all year) and everywhere else was dull winter! People came from everywhere to see this. I felt happy. The next few days I distinctly felt energetically lighter... and still do. It feels easier to have positive thoughts and if negative heaviness arises I am aware of its impermanence.

In short I have found the clearing session very beneficial and thank you very much for this valuable opportunity to release and clear. Increased connection to higher self and meditation has distinctly improved too.

Paolo Yudi – Teacher, London

Life Force Energy

Awaken Your Inner Energy

7 Steps to Health ! Happiness !! Harmony !!!

Close your eyes and imagine a Healthy, Happy and Harmonious life, all around You. Now, open your eyes and smile - all of this is available just around the corner. Whether you're looking for Physical Health, Emotional Well Being, or Harmonious relationships...

Awakening to Your Inner Energy will take you there!!

In this 7 week Home Study Course you will learn:

- What is Inner Energy and why it is most important to have a healthy Energy Body.
- What are your 7 Energy Centers and how there optimum health governs almost every area of your life.
- How you can awaken and take care of these Energy centers called Chakras.
- Yoga postures that maximize the flow of Energy into your Chakras.
- Hand Postures or Mudras that control the movement of Energy in your body.
- Meditation to release the blockages in the Chakras.
- Affirmations to strengthen your Mental body.
- Morning journaling to release your emotional garbage.
- And Much More.....

For more information visit:
http://www.LifeForceEnergyBook.com

Life Force Energy

From Chaos to Peace

7 Steps to Release Your Emotional Stress and Connect to Peace

The stress and chaos in the mind that you experience is the result of the emotional blockages in the Chakras. As we open the Chakras and release these blockages one by one we start experience the flow of positive emotions, positive energy and positive thoughts liberating us from our stress and emotional baggage.

This is a meditation course that will help you release your stress by clearing your chakras. In this course you receive:

- State of the Art Guided Audio meditations to energise your chakras and release the toxins and psychic debris stored in them.
- Hand Postures or Mudras that control the movement of Energy in your body.
- Affirmations to strengthen your Mental body.
- Selfoggio frequencies matching each chakra having a profound affect on healing the Chakra, thereby healing your stress.
- Morning journaling to release your emotional stress.
- And Much More.....

For more information visit:
http://www.LifeForceEnergyBook.com

Life Force Energy

Chakra Healing

The chakras are the main powerhouse of energy that is present in out energy body. They directs the cosmic energy into our physical, mental, emotional bodies and are responsible for our over all well being, health and success. The chakras should be open, rounded and balanced without any blockages. During our lives we collect so much etheric, emotional and mental garbage into our chakras that the flow of energy is constrained. Just like we need to maintain our physical body through regular physical excercise, diet etc, similarly our Energy body in the form of chakras requires regular upkeep and maintenance. This chakra healing helps to balance your chakras and free them of all etheric, emotional blockages.

Chakra Healing Session

I conduct the session on Webinar / Skype and it usually lasts between 45 minutes to an hour. We start with a Chakra meditation using visualisation and sounds for energising each chakra. This helps activate the chakras and the life force energy flowing through them. I then connect you to your higher self after which I start energy transmission using frequencies of higher dimensions resonating in Divine Unconditional Love and one by one I clear all your Chakras of any blockages present in them. In the end I do a download from your higher self that keeps you anchored with your higher self and you start receiving new soul programming and guidance in your life.

For more information visit:
http://www.LifeForceEnergyBook.com

Life Force Energy

Auric Clearing

Cleans your Aura of the auric attachments you have picked up from people, places, times, things and events. Everytime you come in contact with anything you experience its aura at the etheric level. Openings in your auric field can absorb other people's negative energy which can spill your Life Force away and cause you to feel tired and restless. Auric Attachments are blockages of life-force energies. they become "solidified" in the subtle bodies due to stress, trauma, and unresolved emotions such as fear, hatred, self-pity, etc. For good health of the etheric body Auric clearing of these attachments and removal of discarnates and other foreign entities from your field is a must.

Auric Clearing Session

I conduct the session on Webinar / Skype and it usually lasts between 45 minutes to an hour. We start with a Chakra meditation using visualisation and sounds for energising each chakra. This helps activate the chakras and the Auric body. We then connect you to your higher self after which I start energy transmission using frequencies of higher dimensions resonating in Divine Love and one by one I clear all your Chakras of any Auric Attachments present in them. In the end I do a download from your higher self that keeps you anchored with your higher self and you start receiving new soul programming and guidance in your life.

For more Information visit:
http://www.LifeForceEnergyBook.com

Life Force Energy

Raise Your Money Energy

Money is nothing more than Universal Life Force Energy that is exchanged when we give our creativity a physical form as a product or service. It is the exchange of your creative energy with another persons creative energy that Money as we see it in the physical form facilitates. However your ability to attract this energy in your life is greatly hampered by your beliefs and mental programs. These are stored in your energy body as what we call as Karmic Patterns. They are patterns because they are energetic blockages that force you to keep making the same choices and thereby keep you stuck in your current level of wealth and abundance. They prevent you from taking action and more importantly making choices that will RAISE the level of Wealth and abundance you are manifesting in your life.

Some of the Karmic Patterns that block your ability to create more financial abundance are:-

- Undeservingness
- Unworthiness
- Guilt and Shame
- Lack, Limitation
- Poverty Consciousness
- Self doubt, Self sabotage, Self diminishment

With these imprints gone you're life will finally change and become much more easy, enjoyable and fulfilling.

For more information visit:
http://www.LifeForceEnergyBook.com

Life Force Energy

Karmic Patterns Healing

With every thought we create, word we speak and act we conduct Karma is created. This Karma gets stored in our subtle body and guides our psyche and behavior, influences our thought pattern and eventually the choices that we make. As we are a some total of all the choices we have made in the past, we are a sum total of the Karma we created. These running programs, or scripts that we came into this world programmed to experience, learn from and evolve from are the Karmic patterns. Its not the external situations and circumstances so much that create us but our reaction and response to that that determines our success or failure. We can clear our selves of these underlying imprints. When these are cleared, we find that we no longer react to other people's nonsense, can receive clear guidance from our higher selves and live in peace, joy and harmony.

Karmic Healing Session

The Session duration is 45 min to an hour and in this I connect to your higher self and identify the HIGHEST PRIORITY Karmic patterns that require clearing for you. Then I clear these patterns from your consciousness one by one using energy transmissions from the higher universe of Divine Love and Harmony. Your Higher self will guide me to the highest priority issues which are hindering your evolution and cause the greatest fragmentation and suffering in your current life situation.

With these imprints gone you're life will finally change and become much more easy, enjoyable and fulfilling.

For more information visit:
http://www.LifeForceEnergyBook.com

Life Force Energy

FREE BONUSES

Bonus 1: 7 Day Chakra Detox Course
Receive a free video each day to Detox your 7 chakras one by one. Helps releasing the emotional toxins stuck in the chakras and achieve emotional balance and peace of mind.

Bonus 2: Chakra Cards
Colored Chakra cards to help you meditate on Chakras and maintain a healthy energy body.

Bonus 3: Stress Busting Meditation
Receive a powerful meditation that releases your stress and brings your mind that is wondering in Past regrets or Future worries back to the peaceful present moment.

To claim your bonuses

www.LifeForceEnergyBook.com

Made in the USA
Charleston, SC
30 October 2015